Creative Play Exercises

from the book

Soulful Sex:

Weaving Sex, Love & Spirit
into Everyday Life

by Diana Owens

This book is part of the home study course
Soulful Sex: A Course of Sexual Liberation.

For more information about this course,
please visit www.lovingway.net/course

Creative Play Exercises

These exercises are designed to help you learn how to integrate love, sex, and spirit into your everyday life. Let the exercises guide you and be a springboard for launching your own soulful creativity about yourself and your own love life. Be wild, playful, and creative. Take risks! One of the ways we grow is to push ourselves a little and support ourselves a lot.

Most people who are creating a project need certain tools for completing a project easily, efficiently and competently. I suggest the following tools for you on your journey of growth.

1. **Ritual**—Ritual focuses your attention on what you are creating. It brings you support by alligning you energetically and vibrationally with what you want to create.
2. **Breath**—Breath heightens awareness and brings energy to your experience. It's like bringing a magnifying glass to the present moment and your own experience physically, emotionally, mentally and spiritually.

3. **Meditation**—Meditation prepares your heart, body and mind to receive the blessings of each exercise. It puts you in a peaceful and receptive mode to listen to your higher wisdom and inner guidance that can support you in using the exercises for your highest growth.

4. **Truth Telling**—Telling the truth is a spiritual and emotional muscle building exercise. It strengthens you in your understanding of yourself and your ability to express who you are to others

5. **Self Responsibility**—Taking responsibility for whatever is happening and for what your projections are about yourself, others and life is an important and wonderful way of heightening your awareness that your life and your happiness is your own creation. You can create the life you desire. It starts by taking responsibility for what is and then making a choice to go where you want to in your love life and ordinary life.

6. **Presence**—The present moment is all we have. When we are truly in the present moment, we have absolute freedom to be who we want to be and create what we want. Happiness and peace and love is available to us here and now. All we need to do is wake up and be here now!

7. **Openness**—Opening up and expressing feelings is staying with what is most alive in us and magnifying it. Emotions are just energy in motion. As we stay open to identifying and expressing emotions, we stay relaxed and flexible and in the flow of life. This is the path to ecstasy.

8. **Awareness**—Awareness is the key to change and growth. As we become aware of ourselves and our choices, we have freedom. We can continue what we are doing or we can choose to change. A suggestion to heighten awareness is to get a journal and use it to write or draw your answers to these questions. Blessings on your path!

Table of Contents

Exercises for the Spirit

Exercises of Love

Partner Exercises

Exercises in Sexuality

Weaving Sex. Love & Spirit into Everyday Life

Exercises for the Spirit

To me, Spirit means the life force within us and within all of life that tends towards growth, goodness and wholeness. Spirit is what helps us weave sex and love into our own life and our relationships. Spirit is the source of all happiness and peace. The following exercises help us cultivate relationship with Spirit. Since Spirit working within us is subtle, we need to learn to listen and to pay attention to how Spirit communicates to us so that we can follow Spirit's guidance.

Exercise 1: Coming to Terms with Sexuality, Spirituality & Love

Make 3 columns on a piece of paper. Put sexuality at the top of the first column, spirituality at the top of the second column, and love at the top of the third column. Put all the qualities and descriptive terms that are associated with sexuality under the word sexuality in the first column. Do the same with spirituality and love in the second and third column. Then circle all the words that are in at least 2 of the 3 columns.

Notice what sexuality, spirituality and love have in common based on what is circled. What seems to be distinct about these three terms? What is your definition of sexuality? Of spirituality? Of love? Based on your thinking and your experience, what is the relationship between sexuality, spirituality and love?

There is no right or wrong answer to these questions. It is important, though, that you be clear about what your definition is of these three areas of your life and what your relationship is to each of them and what their relationship is to each other. This will help you in doing the rest of the exercises in this chapter.

Names are important in our lives and in our culture to describe our experience and to create a shared form of communication that expresses the meaning we have for our experiences. The philosophy and practice of Tantra aims at imparting the sacred in all of our lives, and especially in our sexuality. For this reason, I have used the Sanskrit names found in tantra practices to describe the sex parts of the man and woman. The man's penis will be described as the vajra, which in Sanskrit means thunderbolt. Another Sanskrit term for penis is lingam, which means light wand. The woman's vagina is called yoni which is Sanskrit for sacred space. The woman's clitoris is called cleo. The name for the anus in both men and women is called rosetta.

The man and the woman in Tantra are called Shiva and Shakti named after Shiva, the Hindu God of Creation, which represents pure consciousness, and Shakti, his partner who represents pure energy or the life force of creation. The union of Shiva and Shakti represents wholeness in life and in each of us. I hope the use of these terms will help you feel and express the reverence for the body, for sexuality and for all of life that is found in tantra practices.

Exercise 2: Creating Sacred Space

Think about the power of intention to create time and space for you to learn and grow. What is your intention for reading this book? What do you want to create through this time and space? Write this in your journal.

Visualize yourself having fulfilled your intention. How are you acting? How do you feel? What are you saying to yourself? Others? How are you interacting with your beloved? Your beloved could be yourself, your life partner, family members, and friends. Write your vision for yourself in your journal.

Draw this vision. Use colors, different media such as magic markers, crayons, chalk, pictures from magazines, pieces of cloth or other materials. Ask your creative mind to express what you desire for your sex and love life and your soul. If you can think it, you can create it. Do it now.

Think about the time you are taking to read this book as a metaphor for your commitment to yourself to love and nurture yourself. When you take time to read this book and do the exercises, will you create a space to support yourself that is nurturing, loving and relaxed? Notice if you can definitely say yes or if your answer is no or maybe. Where will you go in your home that is relaxed, nurturing, loving and supportive of your own growth?

If you don't have a space like this, will you create it? You can use a special corner, a favorite piece of furniture. You can create your own altar where you light a candle when you spend time there. You can put favorite pictures of yourself, your beloved and your spiritual teachers on the altar. You can use music, incense, and flowers. Be creative in designing a space that appeals to all of your senses. Write in your journal to describe your sacred space.

If you have a partner, talk about a special time during the day that you will do creative play. Make an agreement to take this time. If you are single, you might consider finding a study buddy, someone who is interested in sacred sexuality and would like to learn and grow with you. When is the time you will take? How long will you take?

Take your agreement seriously. Do not make the agreement unless you are 100% sure that you can and will keep it. Keeping agreements with yourself or others builds trust. When you break agreements, notice what happens. One of 2 things usually happens. We either go unconscious and lapse back into old habits of putting everyone else and everything else first or something else has a higher priority for us. When we look at how we spend our time, we can see what our highest needs are. How do you think you might block yourself from reading this book and doing the creative play exercises?

How do you plan to deal with and resolve your blocks so you can get what you want from this experience?

Confronting and resolving your blocks is primary in growing the way you want to grow. Go for it!

Rituals are ways of marking time and are very important in heightening your experience. What ritual will you use to begin and end your time of reading the book and doing the exercises? An example would be to light a candle and put your hands in prayer position and bow and use the greeting Namaste which is Sanskrit to mean I honor the divinity in you that is an aspect of myself. Name your ritual. Put it in your journal.

Exercise 3: Meditation - Cultivating Sacred Space Within & Developing the Art of Weaving Sex, Love & Spirit into Everyday Life

If we think of our body as our temple, meditation becomes the purifying agent for keeping the temple of our body clean and of the highest quality. Meditation is also like the guardian of the temple. It allows us to be consistently watchful and observant of where our thoughts go, what our emotions are and what our behavior is.

Through meditation, we can cultivate the observer within, the part of us that is consistently present and aware of all of our functions, and making choices every moment for our highest good.

The following is a very simple meditation exercise I have adapted from the Diamond Heart work I have done. It is called the Kath meditation taken from a Sufi word. It basically helps us focus on the 2nd chakra, the center of our strength, health, and balance. (See the Chakra diagram on page 166 of the book *Soulful Sex*).

Preparation:
Dress in loose fitting clothing.
Create Sacred Space.
Do an opening ritual.

Sit in a way that your spine is straight and your heart and chest are open. You could use a meditation cushion, a straight back chair, or several pillows underneath you.

Creative Play Exercises

Start by putting your hands in prayer position in front of your heart and bowing your head. Bring your head back up to its normal position and place your hands right below your navel, with your thumbs placed over each other and your left hand over your right. Locate a position that is 2 fingers down from your belly button and 2 fingers inside. This area is called the kath and this is the point on which you concentrate. This helps you focus on the center of strength, health and balance. It is the physical center of the body and will help you ground yourself in your body. It will also aid in helping you develop the ability to concentrate.

Breathe normally through your nose and concentrate on your kath. Count your breaths up to 6, then start over again. Watch if your thoughts wander and bring them back consistently and firmly and lovingly to your kath. As you become more comfortable with this meditation practice, you can notice where your mind goes, as a way of learning what your mind attaches to, what it values and seeks to focus on.

Start doing this practice everyday for 10 minutes. Pick a certain time and place and do this regularly. Extend the practice to 30 minutes a day over time. Notice what changes happen, as you become more regular with your practice. What are you learning about yourself and your life through this practice? Write in your journal what changes are happening. Often, you don't notice changes until you stop your meditation. Then you might realize you are more reactive or nervous then when you meditate daily.

If sex, spirit and love are fine threads in the weaving of your life, meditation becomes the master weaver. It helps you develop the strength and peacefulness and awareness and presence to know just how to weave the threads into the finest tapestry, that is seamless, beautiful and better because of the richness of all the individual threads combined.

Soulful Sex

Exercise 4: Breathwork

Aim:

To develop your ability to breathe deeply and to use your breath to intensify your awareness, energy level and pleasure. Deep full belly breathing is essential to relax and to become more aware of the present moment. It also energizes us, helps us move energy and heightens our pleasure. Deep full breathing is essential to learning how to bring your energy up through the seven chakras and to bring pleasure to your sex organs and to your entire body. We can also learn to control the breath and the level of sensations and excitement we have. Further, and knowing how to breathe and control your breath allows you to connect energetically to your partner. As you can synchronize your breath with your partner, you can harmonize and unite your energy.

Preparation:

Create Sacred Space and do an opening ritual.

You can be naked or dressed in loose fitting clothes that do not restrict your breathing.

Position yourself on your back on the floor or on a bed or couch. Put your hands on your abdomen right below your belly button with your finger tips just touching. Extend your abdomen out as if it were a red balloon and you're filling the red balloon up with air. You'll notice that your fingertips separate slightly when your belly is distended. This experience is unfamiliar to many people because we are in the habit of holding our bellies in and chest breathing . This does not allow our breath down into our diaphragm which is what belly breathing is.

Creative Play Exercises

Practice inhaling and filling the belly first and then the upper part of the lungs. On the exhalation, let the belly deflate first then the upper part of the lungs. Continue to practice this with your hands on your belly until you get into the habit of inflating and deflating your belly first. This kind of breathing will give you much more oxygen especially to your extremities, including your head and your sex organs. This will give your more relaxation and more pleasure.

Sit on a meditation pillow or several pillows with your spine straight and your legs crossed in front of you so that your pelvis and hips are higher than your legs. You can also use a straight backed chair for this exercise.

Take a couple of cleansing breaths where you breathe in very deeply and expel your breath strongly on the exhalation several times, like you're forcefully releasing all the old stale energy from your system. Then find a regular rhythm of breathing that is just right for you. Focus on whatever is most prominent about your breath, the rise and fall of your chest and abdomen as you inhale and exhale or the coolness and warmth of your breath as it enters and exits through your nose and mouth. Whatever you focus on, keep bringing your mind back to your breath every time it wanders, noticing where it went and what it focused on when it was gone.

This practice is similar to Vipassana meditation and allows you to develop and strengthen the witness part of you that can observe your experience without becoming so immersed in it that you lose attention. When you can notice what your mind attaches to, you can see what's important to you at the moment. Then bring your mind back to your breath firmly yet lovingly. It is important to not judge yourself when your mind wanders, just bring it back to the breath.

On the exhalation, let your body begin to relax and surrender more and more. Practice letting go more and more with every exhalation. You can progressively go from the top of your head, relaxing every part of your head, then moving down progressively to every body part relaxing more and more and more with each exhalation. On the inhalation, breathe in peace. Make peace into a color. Take the color into the part of your body that you are relaxing. When you have reached your toes, breathe the color of peace into your whole body, intensifying the color with every breath you take, letting the color of peace spill out around you, surrounding you with a bubble of peace that can support and protect you at the same time. When you feel complete, imagine that there is a mirror at the front of the bubble of peace so that only positive energy reaches you and any negative energy bounces back to its owner.

You can use this ritual of protection whenever you feel anxious or need support. We don't relax naturally. We need to practice relaxation and teach our body to relax through repetition.

$\mathcal{E}$xercise 5: $\mathcal{S}$acred $\mathcal{S}$exual $\mathcal{B}$reathwork

You can continue as part of the above exercise or let this be a stand alone exercise.

Breathe in through your mouth as if you're sipping through a straw and exhale slowly through your mouth. Let your mouth and jaw and throat relax. Now take your breath down to your genitals. Focus your attention on your genitals. Imagine that your genitals are breathing the clearest purest freshest air and that the oxygen is not only revitalizing your genitals but tickling them and waking then up to their full potential of pleasure. Exhale out your genitals as well. Give yourself permission to fully enjoy the sensations in your genitals and notice all of the pleasure and other sensations that you're feeling. You might be aware of vibrations or warmth or tingling. Simply notice and be aware of what your experience is.

When you're comfortable with genital breathing, visualize taking the breath from the genitals all the way up to the brain, bathing the brain, then letting the energy flow back down to the genitals on the exhale.

When you are comfortable with taking the energy up to the brain on the inhale, expand it and shoot energy out the top of your head on your inhale, then bring it back down bathing your entire body and being with golden light filled energy on the exhalation.

Exercise 6: Body Blessing Exercise

Aim:
This is a way of acknowledging that Spirit and love are part of the body. Through our intention and our focus, we bless the body and acknowledge that we love our body and see it as Spirit filled.

Preparation:
Give yourself 30 minutes for this. Be nude for this exercise. Create sacred space and do an opening ritual.

Stand nude in front of the mirror with soft lighting or candles and serene heavenly music. Close your eyes and ask that God, Goddess and the angels of healing be with you in your body blessing and give you the strength to love, honor and bless your body in the way that is right for you.

Soulful Sex

Open your eyes. Gaze softly at yourself. Cultivate soft vision, meaning that you look at your entire body and don't try to focus on any one part of to be specific with any details. The idea is to cultivate a soft gaze where you look at yourself as whole, complete and beautiful just the way you are.

Breathe in and out slowly. Look deeply into your own eyes. Begin to see the person you are on a soul level. Start connecting with the life journey that this person standing in front of you has had. Notice all of the pain, challenges, losses, hurts, disappointments that this person has had. Let compassion for this being standing in front of you rise up inside your heart. Let yourself start breathing from your heart and sending love to this person's heart standing in front of you.

Connect your heart to the heart of the person standing in the mirror. Imagine that you are a messenger of the angels to this person standing in front of you. You are sent here to remind this person that they are a child of the universe, perfectly made, wonder filled just as they are. You are here to offer blessing to your whole body and each body part.

Start with your toes and feet. Say, Thank you feet for carrying me so far on my journey of life, and not giving out on me even when I am tired. I bless you and love you just the way you are. Go up to your legs. Say the same thing. Thank you legs for carrying me around and being so strong and enduring. I bless you and love you just the way you are. Go to your genitals. Say something personal and unique like, Thank you genitals for all the pleasure you have given me and the children you have helped me create and the attractiveness to my partners that you have offered me. I bless you and love you just the way you are.

Continue in this same way to each body part until you get to the top of your head. Then look at your body as a whole. Thank your body and bless it with the following or similar words. Thank you so much for being my partner in this life. I know you have done the best you can. I offer you my love and support for your good health, well being and happiness. I bless you and love you just the way you are.

Hug yourself and thank yourself for doing this exercise.

Do a closing ritual.

Becoming Aware of Energy

I have put these exercises as part of Exercises of the Spirit because they help us connect to spirituality.

According to many experts in sacred sexuality, the ability to understand and move energy is a primary skill necessary for both developing and expanding orgasmic energy and transforming it in order to connect to the divine.

The tradition of yoga has given us much help in understanding energy through the chakra system of ancient India. The chakra system describes 7 primary energy centers of our body that affect our physical, emotional and spiritual health and well being.

When these energy centers are blocked or undeveloped, we can get sick physically or have emotional problems or feel confused and out of touch spiritually. When the chakras are open, energy flows freely and we experience connection on all levels that is felt as high energy, vitality, pleasure, radiant health, happiness, peace, fulfillment, creativity and a sense of oneness with all of life and the Divine.

Soulful Sex

The following exercises are designed to help you get in touch with the energy centers themselves and the physical and emotional issues that are connected with each chakra as well as develop a positive affirmation to support the opening and strengthening of each chakra.

Preparation for exercises:
Set aside ½ hour of time for each exercise.
Dress in loose clothing and create sacred space with an opening and closing ritual.

Energy Exercise 1

(Taken from David Yarien and Sandy Anders workshop exercises.
See their contact information at the back of this book.)

Aim:
To experience the difference between tension, relaxation and ecstasy.

Stand in place. Clench your fist as tightly as possible. Hold this for at least 1 minute. Notice how your clenched hand feels.

Do you feel pain, tension, and numbness? This is the experience of tension. How often do you feel this during your day? Are you aware of how much effort and energy it takes to keep up this tension? Where in your body do you tend to tense up like this? Places that often hold this kind of tension are the head, jaw, neck, shoulders, chest, belly, small of back, back of legs, toes.

Do you feel drained after being this tense? This takes energy and effort. As I tell my clients, worrying doesn't help, either physically or emotionally.

Now, sit down and relax you hand. Place it on your lap. Let this hand soften, relax and let go. Feel the softness, relaxation, heaviness or possible lightness in your hand. What does this feel like?

What are the sensations in your hand? Does it feel pleasant?

Is it hard for you to keep your hand this relaxed?

What happens to the other part of your body as you relax your hand? Usually other parts of your body tend to relax when you relax one part. This is called the relaxation response. Relaxation usually takes practice. We don't naturally know how to relax. We need to learn how to relax through practice.

Now, shake your hand and whole arm vigorously for about 30 seconds. Have fun doing this, but don't strain yourself. Put your hand back on your lap. Notice the sensations in your hand now. What are you aware of?

Does your hand feel more alive, warm, tingly, pulsing, electric?

Does it feel more pleasureful than before? How much? This is called the ecstasy response. In this culture, we are usually not taught how to experience ecstasy. In fact, we are encouraged to suppress it in the name of being appropriate and controlled. We can have ecstasy very fully when we use movement, breath, sound and presence to awaken and expand the pleasure in our sexual energy center, and bring this energy up into our heart and up into the spiritual centers.

We will learn how to do this in the following exercises.

00

Soulful Sex

Energy Exercise 2

Aim:
To become acquainted with energy around your hands.

Rub your hands fast, like you are warming up your hands. Do this for 30 seconds. Now place your hands above your head, palms down with an opaque surface like a ceiling above you. Look through your fingers with soft eyes, not gazing at anything in particular. See if you can define energy lines around your fingers. A lot of times, people can see distinct lines around the fingers or energy vibrations around the fingers like when you are driving on a road and you see what looks like a wet spot in front of you with wavy lines rising from it. If you don't see anything different, try different lighting behind the hands.

Energy Exercise 3

(Taken from Anodea Judith's book.
See Appendix at the back of this book for reference.)

Aim:
To become familiar with energy.

Stand in place. Rub your hands together fast. Now place both arms straight out in front of you, one palm facing up, the other one facing down. Now open and close both of your fists very fast 20 times. This will open your hand chakras. Now bring your hands together slowly until they are about 4 inches apart. Notice if you can detect an energy flow between your hands. Many times, people will notice heat or a pulsing energy or a magnetic attraction or repulsion or an electric feeling or a sensation of fullness. Play around with this. Form an energy ball with your hands. Bring your hands close together without touching, now take them as far apart as possible and still feel a connection. Notice when you stop feeling this connection.

What is this like for you to feel this? What do you make of it? Does the concept of chakras make sense to you?

Energy Exercise 4

Aim:
To become familiar with the 7 chakras and your experience of them.

Preparation:
Set aside 1/2 hour for this exercise. Dress in loose clothes or be nude.

For the first 3 chakras, use Osho Chakra Breathing Meditation music (See www.newearthrecords.com) or drumming music; for chakras 4-7 use heart and etheric music.

Stand in place to do this exercise with your feet about shoulder length apart, your legs relaxed and your arms at your side.

Breathe deeply and slowly to do this exercise.
Close your eyes half way so that you are focused inside.
Begin by placing 1 hand at the base of your spine where your tailbone

is. Place your other hand on your pelvis to get in touch with your root or first chakra. Start pulsing, bending your knees up and down, feeling your feet. Let your energy move up into your hips, pelvis and genitals. Enjoy the sensations there and expand the pleasure you're feelings by moving and dancing letting yourself feel and express your sexuality and your life energy. The color is red. Bring this color up into your feet, legs and into the base of your trunk and spine. The genitals are the body parts connected with the 1st chakra, and the prostate, testes and ovaries are the glands connected with this center. The issues are survival, security, sexuality, and prosperity. Ask yourself, Do I feel secure and safe in the world. Do I feel passionate and sexual? Do I take risks or do I feel afraid and weak and untrusting of others and myself? Affirmation to strengthen the root center is I am safe and secure in this world. I am sexual and passionate about living. I trust in the goodness of life to carry me through.

Bring your hands up to your abdomen. The 2nd chakra is located here and in the womb, spleen, liver, low back and hips. Move your hips. Breathe into your pelvis and belly and hips. Let this energy move through this area energizing, enlivening and bringing health to the organs and body parts of this area and of your entire body. The color is orange. Imagine a brilliant orange sun setting over the ocean. Let that flowing and warm orange energy bring aliveness and fluidity to your pelvis and abdomen entitling you to pleasure, joy, good health and balance. Ask yourself Do I embrace my feelings openly and fully? Do I hold back my feelings and end up feeling numb or depressed? Affirm for yourself: I embrace all of my emotions and accept health, balance and wellbeing into my life. I am a magnificent, healthy and fully alive and balanced human being.

Bring your hands up to your solar plexus, right below the rib cage and ending at the belly button. Breathe into your solar plexus. The color is yellow, the element is fire. It's associated with the pancreas, stomach, gall bladder and liver and the assimilation of sugar and digestive functions.

Creative Play Exercises

It's connected with power, energy and our identity. Imagine a brilliant sun rising in your solar plexus, giving you the power to be yourself, and bestowing on you the blessing of living life fully. Ask yourself the question Do I feel powerful and in charge of my life and clear about who I am? Do I feel weak, confused, tentative and ambivalent? Affirm for yourself: I am a powerful and magnificent human being filled with life, love and goodness.

Bring your hands and breath to your heart. The color here is green, the element is air. It is connected to the thymus gland, the heart, lungs, and circulatory, system. The attitudes are of happiness, joy and delight, knowing what and who make your heart sing. Ask yourself, do I feel loved, loving and lovable or do I feel depressed, alone, and cut off? Imagine yourself and your heart as a beautiful rose, opening to all of life, fully blossoming showing your own unique beauty, delighting in being alive. Affirm I am love. I am connected and in love with life and all beings. Love connects me to the infinite and makes me whole.

Take your hands and your breath up to your throat area. The color is blue and element is sound. It is connected with the thyroid and parathyroid glands and the respiratory system. It has to do with your ability to express yourself and your feelings truthfully and openly. It also connects to your creativity. Ask yourself, do I live in integrity, expressing my truth and my creativity or do I repress myself and feel misunderstood and invisible? Imagine a blue healing light transforming the energy of your throat, mouth, and jaw so that you speak your truth and create from your center naturally and effortlessly. Visualize yourself living in integrity. Affirm I speak my truth and live in integrity. I express myself as creatively as possible.

Take your hands and your breath up to the middle of your forehead. The color is violet and the element is light. It is associated with the pituitary gland, the brain and the nervous system. It has to do with intuition, psychic perception and imagination. Ask yourself do I trust my intuition and psychic perception and act on it in my life or do I doubt myself and second guess my impulses and inner guidance? With your eyes closed, look upward to your brow chakra. See the image of a candle flame and many colors. Be open to any images that come. Move to however the energy wants to move you. Affirm I follow my inner guidance as an expression of divinity. I am able to discern the good.

Take your hands and breath to the top of your head. The element is thought or spirit. It is associated with the pineal gland, the brain, the central nervous system and the whole endocrine system and the rhythm of waking and sleeping. The color is white or gold. Key issues are enlightenment and connection with the divine. Ask the question Do I feel at one with life and all that is or do I feel despairing, disconnected, and without a spiritual direction? Take your attention and breath to the crown and move to the energy. Imagine that golden sunshine rays of light are flowing down into you and you are opening to receiving this energy and sending your gratitude and love down into the earth on your exhalation so that you become the bridge between heaven and earth. Affirm I am one with all that is. God in me, as me and through me.

At the end of this exercise, keep your eyes closed. Breathe deeply. Notice what sensations you are aware of in your body. Scan all of your chakras from your base or root chakra to your crown. Notice what chakras are open and flowing. Are you aware of sensations in every chakra or are some chakras numb or without sensation. When you focus your awareness on your chakras, can you sense into them or are there areas that feel invisible to you? How does this relate to your early life and your development? Are there areas that you know you shut down or did not develop in your life? Can you see how the chakra system can help you develop in these areas? How might you take what you learned from this exercise and develop the chakras that need to be developed?

Creative Play Exercises

Exercises of Love

Thich Nhat Hanh talks about love as being the intention and capacity to offer joy and happiness. He also indicates that true love includes compassion and equanimity or the ability to let go and be with what is. (*Teachings on Love* by Thich Nhat Hanh, pp. 4-8). The following exercises help us develop love for ourselves, our partner and all those who are in our lives.

Exercise 1: Heart Opening Experiences

Name three of the most heart opening experiences of your life. What was the impact of these experiences on you, then and now?

Name qualities that these experiences have in common. Are any of them loving, spiritual or sexual in nature?

We can't make these kinds of experiences happen, but we can cultivate the qualities in ourselves that attract these experiences to us.

Name one quality that you will cultivate in yourself to attract more of these experiences to you? What will you do to cultivate this quality?

Exercise 2: Becoming Your Own Best Lover

(Adapted from *The Art of Everyday Ecstasy* by Margot Anand)

It is common knowledge that if we don't love ourselves, it is very hard to offer others love. I find this is especially true when in an intimate relationship. Loving myself helps me stay away from blaming my partner if I don't get what I want in the relationship. It also helps me stay out of feeling guilty, responsible and wrong when my partner gets angry with me or blames me for something s/he doesn't like.

Aim:
The following exercise is a fantasy about loving yourself. Treat this lightly. If something doesn't fit, adapt your own imagery to create whatever feels wonderfully loving, filling and affirming to you. The idea is to recognize yourself as precious, priceless in value and lovable beyond compare. Enjoy the process!

Preparation:
30 minutes of undivided time for yourself.
Dress in uncomfortable clothing or nothing at all.
Create Sacred Space and do an opening ritual.

Put yourself in a comfortable position either sitting or lying down, but be sure to create a way of not falling asleep. Take a couple of deep breaths, exhale strongly a couple of times, then come to a normal natural rhythm of breathing that is just right for you. As you breathe in, ask your spirit guides and God and the angels to be with you and ask that only good come from this experience and that this be for your highest good and healing.

Focus on your breath and whatever is most prominent about your breathing. On the exhale, let go and allow yourself to relax more and more. On the inhale, breathe in light and love. Make love into a color and breathe it into your heart, and expand it so that the color of love fills your heart, and flows through every blood vessel and artery and saturates every cell and every organ of your body. Let this color of love flow out around you surrounding you with a bubble of love light. Within this bubble, begin to bring to mind all the people, animals and aspects of nature that you have loved and that have loved you. It could be anything from a sunset, to the birth of your children, or an exquisite love affair you had or a favorite fantasy you have of loving and being loved or being in an exquisite place where you feel free, safe, loved and loving.

Begin to focus on one memory. Breathe it in as fully as possible. Experience the way you are loving. You might have a very open heart. You might be crying or kissing someone or screaming in ecstasy or very still and quiet. Notice what you are doing, what you are saying. Who is with you, what they are doing or saying. Notice all that you see, hear, smell, taste, and feel in your body.

When one memory feels finished, go to the next. And then the next. Feel how full of love you are and how much love you have given over the years. Now, imagine that all of these lovers or sources of love have gathered around you and are telling you one at a time how lovable, valuable, precious and exquisite you are!! In other words, they are entitling you to love. They are saying, each in their own way, "I Love You! You are wonder filled, lovable, valuable, special, priceless beyond compare. No one else in the world is like you. I love you sooo much. You are irreplaceable. The world would not be the same if you were not in it. You add something to the world that no one else does. You are my Beloved in whom I am very well pleased!!! Thank you for Being here and Being in my life." Add your own words, images, feelings, and sensations so that you feel full of love.

Soulful Sex

One special person comes out of the group and invites you to meet your own Beloved, the one designed to love you more than anyone else, the one you are to have the most passionate love affair of your life with, the one you love deeply, fully, and unconditionally. Your companion takes you to a beautiful room and introduces you to your Beloved. It is you. You now have the opportunity to make love to yourself in as full and open and loving a way as possible. You begin to see the exquisite qualities of the one in front of you who is you. You begin to fall in love with this person. Notice all of your wonderful qualities. Begin to tell this person who is you how much you adore them, love them appreciate them. Begin to make love to them in your own way. Notice what it is like to love them, to see yourself from the inside out as your lover, your friend your partner in life, your companion. Look into your own eyes and see yourself with compassion and love. Wish yourself, love, joy, happiness, well being, and freedom from suffering, good health and peace. Now embrace yourself. Offer yourself something as a sign of your love for yourself. Remember that when you think of this sign, it will be a reminder to offer yourself love, to come home to yourself as your own best friend and true love.

Think of one way you can give to yourself today to extend this love to yourself. Make an agreement that you will do one kind thing a day for yourself as a sign of your love and your commitment to loving yourself. Give yourself a big hug; Take yourself into your own heart. Come back to the room being all that you are and all that you are becoming.

Partner Exercises

It is preferable for you to have a partner to do these exercises with. This person can be a friend or someone interested in learning more about sacred sexuality or your primary partner. See if you can find a "study buddy" for these experiences. If you don't have a partner, do the exercises anyway, using yourself as your best and primary partner. Use a mirror for the eye gazing exercises.

Exercise 1: Creating Sacred Space

(Taken from workshops created by Margot Anand and Steve & Lokita Carter. See Appendix at the back of this book for information.)

Aim:
To create a space that is attractive, loving, sacred, and safe in which you can be yourselves and share fully with each other.

Preparation:
Take a shower, preferably together with your Beloved. Dress in beautiful, sensual clothing. Put perfume or essential oil on your body.

Create a sacred space defined just for you. You might have a cloth on the floor with pillows for each of you, candles and flowers in the middle and symbols of your spiritual guides such as Jesus, Mary, Buddha, Quan Yin etc. Put on your favorite music to make love to.

Soulful Sex

Do the following ritual to start. Sit in front of each other. Put your hands in prayer position. Bow to each other. Say the words, "Namaste, I honor the Divinity in you that is an aspect of myself." Close your eyes. Center yourself in love. Spend a few minutes with your eyes closed breathing into your heart, opening to loving yourself. Visualize yourself as a bright shining love light, here to reflect back the amazing beauty and preciousness of your partner to her. When you feel ready, open your eyes and see this person, sitting before you as your beloved partner. Begin to see this person as the embodiment of love itself. Start to see your own role as bringing love to this person and showing your partner what an exquisite and precious human being they are. It is also important to see yourself as a crucible, ready to receive your partner's love with your heart fully open and appreciative of all your partner has to give. Remember that in this moment the two of you are each other's Beloved, here to bless each other with love, showering each other with the gift of your precious attention and appreciation. Treat your partner as your queen or king to pay homage to.

Men, start with sharing a gift of appreciation with your beloved partner. You could present her with a real gift you have chosen to honor her or an imagination gift that you know would please her (a cruise to Hawaii on your very own cruise ship with a staff who are hand picked to meet her every need. Use your creativity to design just the offering that would please her totally.) Then offer her a blessing of appreciation for certain qualities that are connected to 2 of her chakras. For example, you might say, I honor your 3rd eye for all the wisdom you bring to me from your intuition. Place your hand on her 3rd eye when blessing her. You might then pick her 4th chakra, placing your hand over her heart, saying how much you value the love she gives from her heart to you and everyone she meets. When you're finished, reverse roles. The woman becomes the giver, sharing a gift, then blessing your partner by appreciating qualities in 2 of his chakras, and placing your hands on each of those chakras. Remember that you are here to bring this man your love and bathe him in your appreciation and nurturing. When you feel complete, go to the next part of this exercise.

Share your intention or desire for this exercise. What do you want to create here for yourself and your relationship? Then what are you afraid of? Then, what are your boundaries? Your boundaries are limits you have in order to feel safe and comfortable. They can be ways in which you won't act or things you need or want in order to feel comfortable. An example of desires, fears and boundaries is: Your desire might be that you want to be fully loving in this exercise. Your fear might be that you are too tired and might fall asleep or be distracted. Your boundary might be that this not end in intercourse. After each partner has shared, continue to Exercise 2.

Exercise 2: Exploring Intimacy

(Adapted from an exercise done by Sally Valentine
at the 2006 AASECT Conference)

Aim:
To develop your understanding of the meaning of intimacy for yourself and your partner, and to practice being intimate.

Preparation:
Set aside 15 minutes for this exercise.

Sit in front of each other. Decide who will be the talker first and who will be the questioner first. Look into each other's eyes as you are doing this exercise.

The questioner will ask a repeating question by asking the same question over and over again for 5 minutes. Use a timer or a watch so you can stop your partner at the end of 5 minutes. At the end of each answer that your partner gives, say thank you to show appreciation and respect for what your partner has said, then ask the same question again. Try to vary how you say the question so you can emphasize different parts of the question each time you ask it. The question is "What is intimacy?"

The talker will have 5 minutes to answer the question. Let yourself say the first thing that comes to mind. This is not a test. Be spontaneous. Stop when you have finished with one answer. Let your partner ask this again. You will probably have many answers. If you don't know what to say, just say you pass.

Then your partner can ask you again. If you finish before the 5 minutes is up, you can ask to stop the exercise. However, it is most effective if each of you take the full five minutes. You may find that one answer leads to the next and that you have a lot more to say about intimacy than you thought.

When the 5 minutes is up, switch roles and the other one ask What is intimacy. There is to be no cross talk during this exercise. The one asking the question needs to be quiet and attentive and let your partner answer the question.

When both of you have finished, process what this was like for each of you. What did you feel during the exercise? What did you learn about yourself and about intimacy?

Complete this exercise by bowing to each other, saying "Namaste, I honor the Divinity in you that is an aspect of myself" and giving each other a big hug.

Creative Play Exercises

Exercise 3: Connecting with The Heart

Aim:
To experience connecting with your partner from your heart, giving and receiving love, being open and vulnerable, and harmonizing your energy with your partner.

Preparation:
Take ½ hour for this exercise.
Dress in loose comfortable clothing.
Create Sacred Space.

Do an opening ritual like what was described in the sacred space ritual. Be sure to do this with each exercise as it gets you in the habit of creating sacred space whenever you are together.

Start by closing your eyes and getting comfortable with yourself. Deepen your breathing, relax progressively more and more on each exhale.

Breathe love into your own heart, giving yourself support to do this exercise. When you're ready open your eyes, and begin to look into each other's eyes with soft eyes, meaning that you don't stare or try to be precise and focused when you look at each other. Instead, soften your gaze and look openly into your partner's eyes, going deep into their soul. At the same time, let yourself open to be seen, allowing the person to see into your soul. Take several minutes for this experience. Continue to breathe deeply and fully, feeling yourself as you look into your partner's eyes so that you continue to come from your own experience and identity.

Soulful Sex

When you are ready, put your right hand over your partner's heart and allow them to place their right hand over your heart. Place your own left hand over their hand over your heart so their hand and your own hand is over your heart. Allow them to place their left hand over your right hand on their heart.

Breathe in love to their heart from your right hand and receive love from their heart through your left hand. Synchronize your breathing so that you are breathing in and out at the same time. Relax into this and continue eye gazing, sending love, and looking into each other's soul, breathing in love and breathing out love. Continue doing this for several minutes.

When you are through with the exercise, give each other a hug, then process what your experience was with the eye gazing and with the giving and receiving love. What were your physical sensations, your feelings, thoughts, memories, associations or judgments? What were you most comfortable with? What were you most uncomfortable with? What did you learn about yourself, each other?

Consider doing this as a daily regular practice.

End this experience with a hug, a thank you and a namaste and bow.

Creative Play Exercises

Exercise 4: Full Body Hug

(Adapted from The Melting Hug as described in Margot Anand's book, *The Art of Sexual Ecstasy*)

Aim:
To experience a hug with your partner that connects with all the chakras. To discover and resolve any inhibitions to hugging your partner fully.

Preparation:
Take ½ hour for this exercise.
Dress in loose clothing or nothing at all. If you choose to be nude, notice what it's like to hug fully with no clothes on.

Start by creating sacred space and do an opening ritual of bowing and saying namaste to each other.

Start by finding your physical and energetic boundaries. Stand across the room from each other. Define who partner A and B is. Partner A stand still and watch as Partner B slowly walks toward you. Notice anything that changes in you to indicate that your partner has reached your boundary. There might be an increase in heart rate or respiration. You might notice yourself getting tense or contracted around the heart or somewhere else in your body.

When this happens, say stop to your partner. This is where your energetic boundary around your body is. This is the place that you are most comfortable in physical relationship to someone else. Many times, this boundary is as big as the length of your arm held out in front of you and to the side of you. Imagine that this boundary goes all the way around your body and is like a fence defining your own personal territory. You have a boundary, no matter who it is that you are with and it is important that you know where your boundary is. If a person is going to come closer to you, it is important that you give that person your permission to come in closer. If you don't, you will end up resenting that person and/or withdrawing from them.

Partner A, experiment with giving your partner permission to come in closer than where your boundary is. Notice what that is like. Now Partner B goes back to the established boundary of Partner A. Partner B now violates Partner A's boundary by coming in without permission. Partner A notice what that feels like. Partner A talk about what this experience was like for you. What did you learn about your boundaries?

Reverse roles and Partner B now stand still while Partner walks slowly towards you. Do the same procedures as listed above and then process it with your partner. What were your feelings while doing this exercise? What did you learn about your boundaries and needs through doing this exercise.

Knowing and sticking with your boundaries is a big issue in any experience of your sexuality. Explore your comfort/discomfort with your boundaries in the next part of this exercise.

Now, stand in front of each other and hug each other in the way you usually do. Complete the hug. Process what you are aware of now about how you hugged. How did you feel while you were hugging? How was your breathing? What body parts were touching? Which body parts were not touching? What sensations did you feel? What was the strength of your hug—soft, hard etc? What was the length of time of your hug? What was the quality of your hug (tender, friendly, sexy, needy, distant)? What did you notice over all about your hug? Many times, people can't answer these questions because hugs are automatic. How aware were you when you hugged?

Begin to hug each other again. As you do this, open your heart as well as your arms. Breathe deeply. Move close to each other. Let all your body parts touch, including your pelvis and genitals. If you're not the same size, don't worry about fitting together in any certain way; just allow all of your body to touch all of your partner's body. Breathe deeply and fully. Take lots of time to receive each other fully. Feel each other's energy and feel your own energy as you do this. Become aware of how you are feeling, the sensations in your body, what you are thinking, Feel yourself opening up to your partner, softening and relaxing into the hug. Feel the luxury of taking lots of time to savor the hug.

After spending a minute or two in an embrace, begin to synchronize your breathing so that you are breathing together, harmonizing your breath. Continue with this for several more minutes. As you are breathing together, feel yourself melting into your partner. Give yourself permission to merge with your partner and receive your partner merging with you. See if you can deliberately let your partner into your personal space. Notice what happens when you do this. When you feel complete, end this experience by expressing gratitude to your partner and bowing and saying namaste.

Now, process this experience with your partner. What felt good and comfortable and pleasurable? What did not? How did you feel about your boundaries? Did you deliberately let your partner into your personal space (inside your boundaries)? Was there any resentment or discomfort about doing this? What did you learn about your ability to give and receive a full body hug? Is there anything that you want to work on further in this area? What specific steps will you take to work on these areas? Can you see ways to use the full body hug to connect more deeply with your partner? What are they?

Soulful Sex

Exercise 5: Variations on the Full Body Hug

Aim:
To explore how to use the full body hug in daily life to deepen intimacy, to resolve conflict and to harmonize your energy in your relationship with your Beloved.

Preparation:
Dress in beautiful sensual clothing and set a romantic atmosphere as part of your sacred space. Take about an hour for the next 2 exercises.

Prepare a space with romantic music where you can dance or hold each other close for a period of time. Do an opening ritual by bowing to each other and saying namaste to each other.

Put on romantic music. Go into a full body hug. Feel yourself melting into your partner, opening your heart and deepening your breathing. As you continue in this position, synchronize your breathing so that you are breathing in and out at the same time. Move slowly together, moving to the music, dancing, swaying, and keeping your bodies connected in all the chakras. Pay special attention to staying connected in the heart and in the pelvis.

Continue to breathe together so that you harmonize your energy. Do not talk during this time. Keep your eyes closed or semi closed, focusing on your breathing and receiving love from your partner on your inhale, then sending love to your partner on your exhale. Visualize a stream of love flowing from your partner's heart to your heart on your inhalation. Imagine it going from your heart to your genitals and on the exhalation send it from your genitals out to your partner's genitals and up to his/her heart.

Creative Play Exercises

Treat this as a meditation and do this for at least 20 minutes. Notice how your energy is over this period of time. If you get uncomfortable, try to vary your position so that you are as comfortable as possible, and yet you stay in the full body hug position. After you feel complete, separate from your embrace, look into each other's eyes, bow, thank each other and say namaste to end the experience.

Process this by talking about what felt good, what felt unfamiliar, what felt uncomfortable. Did any fears or resistance come up for you. What is this connected to? On a scale of 1-10, 10 being top notch and 1 being not at all, rate the level of pleasure and closeness you felt with each other. Is there anything that you would like to change to make it even better for you? Would you like to add this to a daily practice of developing closeness and harmony with each other? If so, what steps will you take to do this?

Exercise 6: Variations on the Full Body Hug for Harmonizing Energy & Resolving Conflict

(Adapted from a Love and Ecstasy Training workshop with Margot Anand)

Aim:
To explore other ways to use the full body hug to harmonize energy and to resolve conflict.

Preparation:
Take ½ hour for this exercise.
Dress in loose clothing or nothing at all.
Select a piece of music that has a strong rhythm to it. Any African drum

music will be great. You can also use Osho's Chakra Breathing Meditation.

Create sacred space. Do an opening ritual. Bow and say Namaste to one another.

Put the music on. Stand back to back with body relaxed and knees slightly bent so that you can pulse, bouncing up and down slightly. Notice how you are feeling about your partner now. How connected do you feel on a scale of 1–10? Rate yourself, 1 being no closeness, 10 being total closeness.

Start synchronizing your breathing.

Start moving up and down at the same time, continuing to synchronize your breath. Emphasize the exhale as you breathe so that you are blowing out strongly. This breath is like the fire breath in yoga only breathe through your mouth.

Now begin to add sounds. Open up your mouth and let out sounds as you continue to breathe strongly. Continue to pulse in time with the music. Continue this pulsing, moving up and down by bending and straightening your knees, keeping your body loose, and breathing in sync with each other.

Take about 20 minutes to continue this exercise. If you want to, you can add focusing on each chakra, starting with the 1st chakra, focusing your awareness and your breath on that chakra, spending about 3 minutes on that chakra, then going to the 2nd chakra etc. until you get to the 7th chakra, then rest and allow the energy to flow down to the 1st chakra again, visualizing golden light filled energy flowing down around both of you soothing you, bringing you love and light and peace and uniting you to each other.

Creative Play Exercises

When you get to the bottom chakra with your visualization, start the process again, breathing together, pulsing your knees so that you are moving in harmony with each other and taking your breath and awareness up to each chakra, ending at the top chakra, letting the energy flow down to your 1st chakra again.

Do this the 3rd time, then rest and breathe together back to back. Notice how you are feeling now. What are your sensations, emotions? How does your body feel? How do you feel energetically? How do you feel about your partner?

Rate your closeness level 1-10 now. Has your closeness improved? Do you feel closer and more loving towards your partner or less close and loving or is it about the same. How do you explain what happened to you and your partner?

Process this experience with your partner. Talk about the following questions: What did you like, not like? What benefited you the most about this exercise? What benefited you the least? What did you learn about yourself and each other from this experience? Are you interested in using this to harmonize your energy regularly or during conflicts? If so, what steps will you take to plan more times for this exercise?

Close this experience with a full body hug, a thank you, a bow and namaste.

Exercise 7: Full Body Contact

Aim:
To explore a way of harmonizing and merging your energy, developing closeness that is easy and pleasant.

Preparation:
Take 20 minutes for this. Dress in loose clothing or nothing at all. Put on soft music. Do this on a bed or couch or the floor. Create sacred space.

Do an opening ritual with a bow and namaste and looking into each other's eyes and opening your heart to each other and beginning deep breathing.

Put yourselves in spoon position with one person lying on your side, your partner in front of you on his/her side with the back of her heart connected to your heart and her pelvis and butt up against your pelvis with your arms wrapped around her and her holding your hands. Feel yourselves relax and melt into each other. Synchronize your breathing. Open your hearts to one another. Make sounds or sighs of pleasure if you like. The idea here is that you are as relaxed and open as possible with one another.

Feel your own energy and each other's energy. Imagine your energy is merging into your partner's, and that you're becoming one energy body. You can say the following prayer taken from Marianne Williamson if it fits your belief system. " Dear God, As we lie here together (or as a morning prayer, as we wake up this morning), may your spirit come upon us. May our minds receive your guidance, may our souls receive your blessing, and may our hearts receive your love. May all those we meet or even think of on this day be better for it. May we serve your purpose in all we say and do. Please show us how. Amen" (Adapted from *Illuminated Prayers* by Marianne Williamson).   Continue to do this for 10 minutes breathing together with your eyes closed, connecting with your energy and your bodies. When you feel complete, continue lying in each other's arms and process this together.

Talk about how this is for you?   What did you like? Not like?   What was pleasurable or uncomfortable for you?   What did you learn about yourself and your partner from this exercise?   Can you see doing this exercise daily possibly in the morning as a way of starting out your day, harmonizing your energy together?   Or maybe last thing at night, would be a good time. What would work for you?

Exercises in Sexuality

A favorite definition of mine regarding sexuality is that it is the grounding of our ability to love. I learned this from David Spangler years ago. Another definition that is used in tantra a lot is that sexuality is our creative life energy. I believe that the highest and best expression of our sexuality is when it is used to express love. The following exercises are designed to help us understand our sexual energy and our feelings, thoughts and memories about our sexuality. The exercises encourage us to learn about our bodies and genitals, and develop an acceptance of how our bodies can give us pleasure and the goodness that resides in our bodies and in our sexuality.

Soulful Sex

Spirituality Through the Body:
The Sacred Space Within

Exercise 1: Body Inventory

Although the body is our partner throughout our lives, many times we don't see it that way. We objectify it and expect it to look a certain way and act a certain way in order for us to accept it and love it. This is an opportunity for you to be very truthful with yourself and your partner and/or friends about what you like or don't like about your body.

Preparation:
Have a hand mirror available and also a full length mirror.

Create Sacred Space and do an opening ritual.

Take about 30 minutes to do this exercise.

Take time in the privacy of your own bathroom or bedroom.

Wash your hands and genitals. Do a nurturing and relaxing ritual first like take a bath or listen to music for a few minutes.

Make an intention that this experience is for your highest good and for your learning. Take your clothes off and look at your body in the mirror. Examine your body from head to toe. Ask yourself the following questions: What parts of my body do I like? Why? Which parts of my

46

body don't I like? Why? Which parts do I consider feminine/masculine? Which parts do I consider sexual, nonsexual. asexual, attractive or unattractive? Why?

Notice how you feel about yourself when you do this exercise. Many times people feel worse about themselves through this experience because they are getting in touch with their judgemental side of themselves which is critical and compares them with the ideal. They always fall short when this happens. The purpose of the Judgemental side of ourselves is to get love. However, it goes about it in the opposite way that is necessary to really get love.

Go back over your body with a more loving and accepting attitude. Decide that you will love and accept yourself just the way you are with the physical characteristics that you have. Decide if there are things about your body that you can and will change. Develop a plan to do this. With the things that you cannot change, decide that you will love yourself with these physical characteristics. Ask yourself, How can I learn to accept my body just the way it is? What is the lesson that I need to learn having been given the body I have? How will I go about learning this lesson? Now, how do you feel? Hopefully, you will feel better and more accepting of your body just the way it is. If you don't, decide that you will do the following exercise daily until you do feel better.

Look in the mirror at your body with soft eyes. Recognize how this body has been your helpmate, partner and friend since the beginning. Thank you body for all the ways it has brought you this far. Offer your body compassion and love and decide on 1 thing you will do for your body today. At the end of the day, check back with yourself to see if you have done it. If so, congratulate yourself. If not, decide what you can do to follow through tomorrow. Call yourself by your own name and say the words I love you to yourself and your body. Notice all the arguments or resistances that come up in loving yourself. Start developing counter arguments that help you love yourself. Say these to yourself every day instead of the judgements.

FOR MEN: Look at your genitals. (There are great diagrams for this in *Male Sexuality* and *The New Male Sexuality* by Bernie Zilbergeld. This exercise is adapted from Male Sexuality, p. 119).

Take time and look at your genitals as if you are seeing them for the first time. Notice the size and shape of your penis, scrotum, testicles, and your perineum (place between your testicles and anus) and your anus. What do you like? Not like? Why? Are you aware of any judgments with the areas that you don't like? Now touch your genitals. See if you can locate the pubic bone above the penis and feel how that feels.

Now, touch your penis, scrotum, and the area behind the scrotum becoming aware of the various sensations that are produced. Press into the perineum and see if you can feel the prostate. This is a very pleasureful spot for men especially when they are aroused. It can be located externally through pressing on the perineum and internally through pressing a finger on the top anal wall. Explore different kinds of stimulation (soft, hard, tickling, nurturing, tender, erotic) and notice what your reactions are. Which areas are more sensitive, less sensitive, more erotic, less erotic? You can lightly touch the outside of your anus and notice what sensations you're aware of here. The anus has a lot of nerve endings and can be a source of much pleasure.

Notice what your sensations are in the aroused and unaroused state. Be curious and use beginner's mind to discover as much about your genitals as you can and how you like to be touched and what turns you on. How do you feel doing this? Are there any memories that come up or associations you make when you do this? What are you learning or becoming more aware of?

Creative Play Exercises

FOR WOMEN: Women, look at your genitals with a hand mirror. Begin by touching the bone and mound of hair that cover your genitals, the mons veneris. Feel the curved bone of the mons through your pubic hair. Move your hands down to your outer vaginal lips or labia and open them to find your inner vaginal lips. Open your inner vaginal lips. Notice the shape of the vaginal opening and its color and texture. Find your clitoral hood and clitoris. Pull back your clitoral hood so that you can see the clitoris itself. Notice if you can see and touch the clitoris apart from the hood. If not, you might not get as much stimulation as if the clitoris is distinctly palpable apart from the hood.

You can touch around the area of your clitoris and try touching the clitoris itself, although it is usually very sensitive to the touch. Notice where you start feeling pleasure when you are touching in and around your clitoris. Find your urethra (urinary opening), your perineum (space between your vagina and anus) and your anus. Gently stroke all around this area including your thighs. Notice what feels good or not. Notice what has little or no sensation. Notice what associations and feelings you have as you continue this touching. Be very curious and learn as much as you can about your responses both physically and emotionally. Take your time and be very gentle with yourself. Push yourself enough to learn something, but not enough to get so uncomfortable you don't want to try this again.

Put a little KY Jelly or other sexual lubricant on your finger if you think you need it and gently insert a finger or two inside your vagina and move it around the rim of the vaginal opening. Notice the sensation of the vaginal tissue and the folds of tissue that surround your finger. The walls of the vagina are very expandable and can accommodate almost any size penis as well as a baby during childbirth. Notice the moisture or dryness of the walls of the vagina. This changes during cycles in a woman's life. Push gently all around against the walls of the vagina and notice where you feel particularly sensitive.

Soulful Sex

Now put your finger half way in and contract your PC (pubococcygeus) muscles around your vagina. You can usually feel the muscles tighten when you do this. If you don't, you might want to do kegel exercises to strengthen the PC muscles, which also help strengthen the intensity of orgasms.

Next, turn your palm facing up and slide your index finger back and up to find your G-spot (GraffenberG-spot or goddess spot). Feel around on the top and front of your vaginal wall to find a small rough patch of tissue about the size of a nickel. This spot usually is sensitive to the touch and when stimulated, it becomes engorged. Women often know they have located it because they feel a desire to urinate when it is touched, It sometimes is hard to find by yourself. You can have your partner locate it for you.

Now slide your middle finger as deep into your vagina as you can. You may be able to feel the end of your vagina. Right before the end, you may be able to feel your cervix. The book *Our Bodies, Ourselves* describes it as feeling like "a nose with a dimple in its center. (If you've had a baby, the cervix may feel more like a chin.)" [p. 274].

You can now take your finger out, examine what it looks like with the vaginal mucus on it. Smell it if you like. Notice how you feel about the smell. You can even taste it. The vagina is self-cleaning, and there are usually more germs on the hands or in the mouth than on or in the genitals.

Men and women, when you are finished, take some deep breaths and thank yourself and your body for this journey. Take your mirror now and look deep into your own eyes and see the being that inhabits this body. Send love to this being and thank yourself for being so curious and courageous to embark on this body journey. End by giving yourself a big hug.

Creative Play Exercises

Exercise 2: Letter to Your Body

Write a letter to your body using the form letter below. Be really truthful about how you feel about your body. Think about your body as a being that you have a personal relationship with, a long history with and lots of feelings about. Use the form letter as a jumping off point. If you want to write other things than what the form letter suggests, do that. After you have finished your letter, put yourself into the position of being your body and write a response back to yourself. Have your body tell you how it feels about you, what it needs from you etc. After you have done both letters, ask yourself what you have learned from this experience and how you will treat your body differently as a result of this exercise.

Dear Body,
I feel angry about
I feel sad/hurt about
I feel afraid/ashamed about
What I appreciate about you is
What I want now is
What I'm willing to do to get what I want is
What I'm learning about myself from you and my relationship with you is

Dear Self,
How I feel about you and your letter to me is...
How I feel about myself is
What I want from you is
Anything else that I want to say to you is
Love,
Your body

Exercise 3: Sharing the Story of Your Body with a Partner

This can be a very powerful exercise. For those of you with partners, consider sharing this together. For those without partners, consider finding someone you trust who you would like to share this exercise with.

Preparation:
Create Sacred Space. Share your desires (what you want from this experience), fears (what you're afraid of) and boundaries (what your needs and limits for your own safety and comfort are. This is a time to tell your partner what is OK with you and what is not. For example, you are not OK with any criticism, and you are not OK with any touching of your body during this exercise).

Do a short meditation together where you look into each other's eyes and synchronize your breathing. This can harmonize your energy and help you feel safer.

Start with a question that you both talk about and answer in whatever way you want to. The question is How do you like to be touched? It is very important that each of you treat the other one's answers with the utmost respect and appreciation, realizing that this is a very vulnerable area for anyone and needs to be treated gently and lovingly. When you are finished, thank each other and tell each other how it felt to talk in this way.

When you are finished, play the following game. Undress each other in the most seductive, loving, validating way you can. Women go first and show your partner how you want to be undressed through how you undress him. After you have undressed your man, invite him to undress you. Men, when you undress your partner, do it in a very loving and complementary and seductive way. Tell her what you like about her body and how beautiful she is to you and how wonderful her body is. Kiss her and caress her as you are undressing her. Look into her eyes and talk to her. Keep reassuring her that you love her body and love to look at her.

Once you are both undressed, each of you can now take a turn standing up in front of each other and sharing what you like about your body and what you don't like and why. Share a little about your history and the emotional wounding that you have experienced through how people have treated you in regard to your body. Talk about your genitals and breasts and any inadequacy you have about them. Men can go first with this exercise. Your partner needs to listen with respect and love until you are done giving you eye contact and her full attention. When you are done, you can tell your partner whether you are open to feedback or not.

Your partner then can tell you how s/he feels about what you said and how s/he feels about your body, especially the parts that you have said you don't like. The partner needs to be very positive. It is important that the partner not give any negative feedback at all, only positive feedback. When you are done, reverse roles and the other person share by standing up and sharing how she feels about her body. At the end of this sharing, talk about how you felt doing this exercise and what you learned about yourself and each other from this experience. Be very honest with each other and yet very sensitive as this exercise puts people in a very vulnerable position. In addition, give each other feedback about how you felt about your partner undressing you. Tell them what you liked about this and if there is anything you would like them to do differently next time. Be sensitive that you don't criticize them as you talk with them. Thank your partner. Give each other a big hug and a namaste salutation to end this experience.

Sexual Muscle Building: Using Kegels for Pleasure & Sexual Skill Building

Aim:

To enhance men's ability to control their urge to ejaculate and to enhance their ability to maintain their erection and to intensify their sexual pleasure.

To increase women's orgasmic pleasure, and to strengthen her vaginal muscles so she can hold the penis more tightly inside her vagina thus increasing sexual pleasure for the couple.

The pubococcygeus, or PC, muscle, is the basic muscle of the pelvic floor and controls the opening and closing of the urethra, seminal canal, vagina and anus. You can locate the PC muscle by starting and stopping the flow of urine when you urinate.

Women are taught kegels during childbirth classes to strengthen the muscles used to urinate after delivery of a baby.

Preparation:

Create Sacred Space.

Do an opening ritual.

Lie on your back on the bed or couch or floor.

Creative Play Exercises

Exercise 1: Contracting the PC Muscle

Identify the PC muscle by contracting your genitals as if you are holding back from urinating. You might feel sensations of tightness or pleasure. This is a sign that you are working these muscles. Begin by rapidly contracting and releasing the PC muscle. Focus on the area between the genitals and anus which is where the PC muscle is located. The sensations are similar to what orgasm feels like, but much more subtle.

Now, bring your breathing into the practice. Inhale, contracting the PC muscle as you do so, while keeping the rest of your body relaxed especially your shoulders. As you exhale, relax the PC muscle. Repeat this for about 3 minutes, using your natural rhythm of breathing. Do not hold your breath, as you either inhale or exhale.

After you're comfortable with this practice, add the visualization of breathing in through the genitals while contracting the PC muscle. Take the breath up to the brain, then back down to the genitals on the exhalation while you relax the PC muscle. Notice how you feel after doing this, especially how your head and brain feel.

After you have practiced this, take the breath up to the top of the head and shoot the energy out to the universe. Then imagine the energy in the form of golden light flowing back down and showering you with blessing and grace flowing all around you purifying and cleansing you of all that is not needed in your life and in your being. Imagine the energy also flowing through you on the inside, bathing your organs and cells in golden light, giving you the grace of health and vitality.

Exercise 2: Pumping

Tighten the PC muscle as you inhale. Then, when you have fully inhaled, hold it for a count of six seconds. Exhale, relaxing the PC muscle and gently bearing down as if you are forcing urine out of your body or having a bowel movement. Repeat this sequence for five minutes.

Imagery can enhance the pleasure of this practice. Women can imagine that you are Queen of the universe and that your vagina is the source of infinite pleasure for your man and that you are irresistible. Imagine that you can draw your man's penis into your vagina at will. You draw your man's penis deep inside you with your sexual muscles, massaging it and caressing it with your powerful juicy sensuous vagina until your man is swollen with excitement, pleasing you fully with his aroused penis.

Men might imagine that the more you use your sexual muscles, the larger and more powerful and more irresistible your penis becomes so that your woman is begging you to come inside her. As you do, she moans with pleasure and your penis responds by increasing in size and strength to please her. Your penis becomes a light wand, bathing her in pleasure and blessing her with love.

Both men and women should contract and relax the PC muscle at least 10-15 times every day for a week. After a week, increase the pumping to at least 30 contractions a day. Keep it going daily. Men and women should see changes in their genital strength and sensitivity within a week. This practice can greatly enhance pleasure and control in lovemaking.

Creative Play Exercises

Relationship as Spiritual Path:
Moving Energy for Pleasure & Transformation

Exercise 1: Pelvic Power

Aim:
To develop awareness of the pelvis, the power and pleasure located in the pelvis, and how to energize the pelvis. To release inhibitions relating to moving the pelvis and experiencing energy in the pelvis.

Preparation:
Set aside 10 minutes daily for this exercise. Create privacy where you can be as uninhibited as possible. Be nude for this exercise or dressed in loose clothing. Put on sexy music with a strong beat that evokes your sensuality like belly dance music, Loreena McKinnit, Book of Secrets or Santana, etc. Create sacred space with an opening and closing ritual. Share desires, fears, and boundaries.

Put sexy music on. Start moving very slowly, putting your energy into your feet, and letting it travel up into your legs and hips and pelvis. Start moving your pelvis around in circles, then forward and back. Let yourself make sounds of pleasure as you move. Breathe through your mouth fully and rapidly. Then start breathing through your genitals. Allow yourself to make your sounds louder. Laugh, sigh, moan and groan, scream.

Let your throat open as well as your hips and pelvis. Move by letting your pelvis lead the way. Be creative. See if you can find pelvic moves that you haven't made before. Experiment with thrusting your pelvis forward. Be deliberately seductive and sexual.

Notice how you feel when you do this. What sensations do you have? What are your feelings and thoughts? Notice if there are any moves you won't let yourself make? Deliberately let yourself get turned on and experience pelvic pleasure. See if you can stretch yourself and go beyond what your normal comfort zone is.

When you feel complete, stop and stand in place or lie down. Notice how you are feeling throughout your entire body. What sensations are you aware of throughout your body? In your pelvis? Breathe into your pelvis. Take your attention to your pelvis; go inside your pelvis as if you are visiting for the first time. What are you aware of? Where are the sensations strongest, weakest? Is there pleasure, pain, or numbness? What do you see, hear, smell, and taste? If your pelvis could talk now, what would it be saying to you? Did you have any associations or memories as you were doing this? What did you learn from doing this experience?

Thank yourself and your body for doing this experience and complete it with a closing ritual like hugging yourself or saying namaste to yourself and/or your partner.

Exercise 2: Pelvic Rock

(Adapted from *The Art of Sexual Ecstasy* by Margot Anand)

Aim:
To learn to heighten energy and pleasure in your pelvis.

Preparation:
Wear loose fitting clothes or nothing at all. Create privacy. Take 15 minutes for this. Do an opening and closing ritual. Share desires, fears and boundaries.

Lie on the floor with your knees bent, and your feet close to your buttocks, shoulder width apart and your arms at your side. With one of your hands, feel the space underneath the small of your back. Put your hand back down at your side. Now, on the inhalation let your lungs and diaphragm expand and push your abdomen out slightly. On the exhalation, let your abdomen soften and the small of your back flatten.

On your next inhale, breathe in fully and allow the space under the small of your back to increase. On the next exhale, flatten your back and let your pelvis tip up toward your head.

On the next inhale, allow your pelvis to tip back toward your feet in a slight rocking motion. Keep the rest of your body relaxed as you do this. When you feel comfortable with this motion, start sexual breathing through your mouth on both the inhalation and exhalation. Inhale as if you are sipping water through a straw to the count of 4. On the exhale, breathe out through your mouth to the count of 4, relaxing your mouth and jaw.

On the next inhale, continue the sexual breathing, tighten your PC muscle and hold it to the count of 4 as you rock your pelvis back toward your feet, On the exhale, bear down with your PC muscle, tip your pelvis toward your head and flatten your back. Continue this motion until you are comfortable with it including the sexual breathing, tightening and relaxing your PC muscle, and pelvic rocking. When you feel complete with the rhythm and the motion of this exercise, stop your motion and lie still. Breathe deeply and notice what sensations are in your pelvis. Would your describe your sensations as pleasurable, neutral or negative? Does your pelvis feel more alive? Are you more aware of your pelvis through this exercise? If there is not more pleasure or aliveness or awareness in your pelvis, what do you think you need in order to create this? What are you willing to do to create this?

A lot of times, this exercise takes practice to develop the sensations and vibrations in the body. It's a way of waking the body and the genitals up. Waking up the body sometimes takes time, especially when these experiences are new. The body learns its responses. Although our sexual energy and sensations are natural, if we don't use them, they become weak from disuse. Practicing the art of sexual pleasure is necessary to develop and strengthen the capacity for pleasure.

Exercise 3: Moving Energy Through the Chakras

(Adapted from Margot Anand's books)

Aim:
To discover how to move and direct our sexual energy. When we learn how to move this energy through the center of our body through all 7

chakras from our base chakra to our crown chakra, we actually bathe all 7 endocrine glands with energy. These glands include the sex glands, adrenals, pancreas, thymus, thyroid, pituitary, and pineal glands. They regulate the body's health and sending sexual energy to them regularly as well as sending them an increased supply of oxygen through our deeper breathing patterns gives us increased vitality and aliveness and health.

Preparation:
Take ½ hour for this. Create privacy and a sacred space. Dress comfortably or undress. Do an opening and closing ritual. Use the music by Osho called Chakra Meditation for the entire exercise or some other rhythmic earthy music for the 1st 3 chakras, and heart and etheric music for the last 4 chakras. Lie down on the floor or a bed or a specially prepared space.

Start with sexual breathing, breathing in through your mouth like you're sipping through a straw and relaxing your jaw and mouth on the exhale. Add kegels and pelvic rocking. Tighten your PC muscle on the inhale as you enlarge your belly letting air fill up your diaphragm. At the same time tip your pelvis back toward your heels and slightly arch your back. On the exhale, flatten your back, bear down with your PC muscle and tip your pelvis up toward your chin. If you feel shaking or vibrating throughout your body, this is a good sign that energy is building up and moving through you. If you don't feel any energy vibrating, that's perfectly OK. Whatever your experience is, is just fine. There is no right or wrong with this experience, just your way.

Place your hands over your 1st chakra by placing them at the very lowest point of your trunk where your pubic mound is located. On the exhale, start chanting the Sanskrit word or mantra that connects with the first chakra which is Lam. The Hindu yogis believe that the sounds that Sanskrit words elicit intensify our energy vibrations. This is also a way of connecting with a very powerful spiritual tradition that is thousands of years old. Continue the inhalation by breathing like you're sipping through a straw.

As you continue your pelvic rocking and kegel exercises and sexual breathing, focus on your first chakra where your hands are placed and notice what the physical sensations are, what emotions are there, and what thoughts, memories or associations are present. This is the chakra connected with survival, sexuality, security, strength and the color red. Do not try to change anything. This is simply an exploration. Take your awareness and curiosity and fascination to the first chakra for your learning.

After several minutes of exploring the first chakra, take your left hand up to your 2nd chakra and on the inhalation, bring your energy up from the 1st chakra at the base of the trunk and spine and take it up to the 2nd chakra in the belly right below the belly button. Move your right hand right above your body from the location of the 1st chakra to the location of the 2nd chakra on the inhalation and back down to the 1st chakra on the exhalation so that you're drawing the energy up through the chakras with your attention, your breath and your hand. The 2nd chakra is connected with balance, flow, emotions, physical health and strength and the color orange. On the exhalation, chant the Sanskrit sound Vam. What sensations, feelings, and associations do you have with this chakra?

Do this for several minutes, then move your left hand up to your 3rd chakra at your diaphragm, right below your rib cage and down to your belly button. On the inhalation continue your sexual breathing, pelvic rocking and kegels and take your right hand from your 1st chakra up to the 3rd chakra, hold it, then release and drop your hand down to your 1st chakra again on the exhalation. Chant Ram on the exhalation. This chakra is connected with power, identity and the color yellow. Notice what sensations, feelings, thoughts and associations you have with this chakra.

After several minutes, move your left hand up to your heart area. On the inhalation take your right hand, following your breath and your attention up from your 1st chakra, through the 2nd and 3rd chakras and to the 4th chakra, hold it, then drop your hand down through the chakras to your 1st chakra. On the exhalation, chant Yam. This chakra is connected to love and the color green. What are your sensations, feelings, thoughts, memories, and associations?

After several minutes, move your left hand up to your throat, your 5th chakra. On the inhalation, take your right hand, following your breath and your attention up from your 1st chakra through the 2nd, 3rd, and 4th chakras to the 5th chakra, hold it, chant Ham on the exhalation, and drop your hand down through your chakras to your 1st chakra again. Remember to continue your sexual breathing, your kegels, tightening on the inhale, and releasing on the exhale, your pelvic rocking and your chanting. This chakra is connected with communication and self-expression and creativity and the color blue. Again, ask yourself what are your sensations, feeling, thoughts, memories, and associations. Does this chakra feel unique, compared to the other chakras? See if you can find a distinct quality in each chakra that seems different from the other chakras.

After several minutes, move your left hand up from your throat to your 3rd eye in the middle of your forehead. On the inhalation, take your right hand from your 1st chakra, move it through each chakra until you get to the 6th chakra, holding it, then on the exhalation, chant Om, release your hand and take it back down through the other chakras to your 1st chakra. This chakra is connected with inner vision and intuition and the color violet. What are your sensations, feelings, thoughts, memories and associations? What is distinct about this chakra?

After several minutes, move your left hand to the 7th chakra right at the top of your head. Rest your left hand lightly at the top of your head. Take your right hand up from your 1st chakra through all of the chakras noticing sensations as you move through the chakras to the 7th chakra, holding it, being silent in that there is no sound for this chakra, then moving your attention, breath and hand back to down through all the chakras to the 1st chakra. This chakra is connected with divinity and oneness with all that is and the color white or gold. What are your sensations, feelings, thoughts, memories and associations? Is there anything distinct about this chakra for you?

Take your left hand down to your base or primal chakra and continue breathing through all the chakras bringing both hands up through the chakras with every inhalation, ending at the crown chakra, then back down through each chakra on the exhalation. If you can't do it on 1 breath continue your breathing taking your awareness, breath and hands up through the remaining chakras with each inhalation and down through the chakras on the exhalation. Be sure to include the sexual breathing, pelvic rock and kegels with this exercise.

When you feel complete, rest your hands at your side, come back to a normal breathing pattern and notice what are your sensations, feelings, and thoughts and associations in your body in general and in each chakra in particular. Where does your energy feel the strongest, weakest, numbest? Is there more pleasure and aliveness in your body? Where?

Congratulate yourself for a job well done. Give yourself a big hug and end this exercise.

Exercise 4: Heightening & Expanding Sexual Energy Through the Chakra Channel

Aim:
To learn how to intensify and hold sexual energy and how to move it in order to intensify the experience of energy in the other chakras

Preparation:
Take 1 hour for this. Create privacy and a sacred space. Be nude if possible or dressed in a robe or sarong or loose fitting clothes. Put on Chakra Meditation music by Osho or other sexy music.

This exercise is the same as the previous one only it involves stimulating yourself sexually and moving the energy through the chakras 3 times before you allow yourself to have an orgasm. If you get to the point of orgasm before this, stop all stimulation and do a kegel where you tighten your PC muscle and send your energy up through your heart to your brain and your crown chakra.

Do an opening ritual. Share appreciations, desires, fears and boundaries with yourself. Start in a comfortable position on your back. Start sexual breathing, breathing in through your mouth like you're sipping through a straw and exhaling through your mouth, relaxing your mouth and jaw. Start kegels and pelvic rocking where you tighten your PC muscle on the inhale and rock your pelvis back toward your feet, and on the exhale, release and bear down with your PC muscle and tip your pelvis up towards your chin and flatten your back. Let yourself make sounds of pleasure and enjoyment as you are doing these movements. Let your mouth and jaw become loose and relaxed. Also, stay relaxed throughout your entire body. The key to heightened pleasure is the ability to relax in high states of arousal.

Begin caressing yourself all over, slowly and sensuously. Give yourself lots of time to show yourself much love. Make this a sacred act of making love to yourself, finding just the places on your body that feel pleasure and want your touch and nurturing. Notice what sensations you are aware of, what emotions you are having, and what thoughts, memories or associations you may be having. Stay present to yourself and your experience. Treat this as a meditation. If your mind wanders, notice where it went and bring it back to your experience firmly yet lovingly.

After you have lovingly caressed yourself all over, begin to focus on your genitals and breasts or other parts of your body that arouse you. Find just the stimulation that arouses you and brings you pleasure. Do not be goal oriented with this experience. Simply stay in the moment and enjoy the experience. Focus your awareness and your breathing on your first chakra at the base of the spine. This is the center of survival, security, sexuality, pleasure and the color red. Breathe in through your genitals, yet continue inhaling as if you're sipping through a straw and exhaling through your mouth, relaxing your jaw and making pleasureful sounds.

Continue doing kegels, tightening your PC muscle on the inhale and releasing and bearing down on the exhale. As your pleasure and arousal increases, you may not want to relax and bear down with your PC muscle on the exhale, but it is important to do this because this allows you to actually build pleasure without releasing it.

Stay with the 1st chakra for several minutes, then as you continue to stimulate your genitals, breasts or other areas that help you become aroused, bring your attention and breath to the 2nd chakra, the area of your belly and your genitals. The color is orange and qualities are physical health, vitality and emotional flow. Continue breathing into this area, doing pelvic rocking and kegels. Notice your sensations, feelings, thoughts and associations.

Stay with the 2nd chakra for several minutes, that as you continue to stimulate yourself, move your attention and breath to the 3rd chakra, in the area of your diaphragm right below your rib cage. This is the center of your power, your identity and the color is yellow. Breathe the energy and pleasure and arousal that you are feeling into this area. Notice what your sensations, feeling, thoughts and associations are.

Stay with the 3rd chakra for several minutes, then as you continue to stimulate yourself, move your attention and breath to the 4th chakra, your heart center, the center of love. The color is green. Breathe the arousal and pleasure you're feeling into this area. Notice what your sensations, feelings, thoughts and associations are.

Stay with the 4th chakra for several minutes, then as you continue to stimulate yourself, move your attention and breath to the 5th chakra, your throat center, the center of communication and creativity. The color is blue. Notice what your sensations, feelings, thoughts and associations are.

Stay with the 5th chakra for several minutes, then as you continue to stimulate yourself, move your attention and breath and energy of arousal to the 6th chakra, the 3rd eye center in the middle of your forehead, the center of inner wisdom and intuition. The color is violet or purple. Notice what your sensations, feelings, thoughts and associations are.

Stay with the 6th chakra for several minutes, then as you continue to stimulate yourself, move your attention and breath and energy of arousal to the 7th chakra, the crown center at the top of your head. This is the center of your connection with the divine and with all of life. The color is white or gold. Notice what your sensations, feelings, thoughts and associations are.

Once you have gotten to the crown center, stop your sexual breathing and your sexual stimulation. Breathe normally. Relax and let your energy slowly flow down your body from your crown to your pelvis and the base of your trunk and spine. You might visualize golden white light flowing down all around your body and also filling the whole inside of your body. Imagine yourself bathed and nurtured and embraced by this golden white light as if you become the light. You can think or say the mantra out loud "The light of love is flowing in me, through me and as me." Take about 2 minutes to get to the first chakra again. Let the golden white light flow down into your arms and hands and legs and feet as well.

When you're ready continue this exercise again, starting by stimulating your genitals again, doing deep, rapid sexual breathing, pelvic rocking, kegels and making pleasure filled sounds. If you get to the point of orgasm, stop and breathe deeply, tighten your PC muscle and take your energy up to your brain. Men, you will learn other skills to stop the urge towards orgasm and ejaculation later in these exercises.

When you are done raising your energy to your crown center 3 times, you can let yourself have an orgasm. If you do this, take your orgasmic energy up to your brain and your crown and shoot it out to the universe. Then let it come back to you and bathe you with love, ecstasy and bliss.

When you feel complete with this exercise, simply lie still with your eyes closed, feeling the sensations throughout your body. Notice what sensations, feelings, thoughts, memories or associations you are aware of now. Take some time with this. You might be feeling a lot of energy flowing throughout your body. Don't try to control it. Let it vibrate. Allow your body to shake or tremble or move in whatever way it tends to.

Creative Play Exercises

When you are ready, think about how the experience of each chakra was as you brought your sexual energy to it. What did you learn about each chakra and your capacity to feel the feelings and qualities associated with each chakra? If you had an orgasm, how was it different than your typical orgasm? If you did not have an orgasm, how did that feel for you? What did you learn about yourself through this exercise?

When you feel complete, hug yourself, thank yourself for doing this exercise, share gratitude and appreciation for yourself and complete the experience.

Exercise 5: Chakra Flow for Couples

(Adapted from the Breath of Love exercise in
Steve & Lokita Carter's workshop Timeless Loving.)

Aim:
To facilitate couples awakening their chakras and connecting them with each other; to balance male and female energy in the couple and in the individual; to intensify feelings of closeness with each other and to prepare for lovemaking.

Preparation:
Take about 1 hour for this exercise.
Dress in beautiful sensual clothing like a sarong or lingerie or your favorite outfit. Create sacred space. Have meditation cushions or pillows or chairs to sit on. Choose rhythmic music for the chakra breathing like Osho's Chakra Meditation music and sensual rhythmic music for the

second part of the exercise like Tantric Sexuality by New World Music.

Start by doing an opening ritual, bowing, saying namaste to each other, and sharing what you love and appreciate about each other. Then, talk about you would like from this experience, what any fears or reservations are and what your needs for support are. Put on some rhythmic sensual music. Dance by yourselves and then together. If you are not comfortable dancing, try any other aerobic exercise to get your energy going. Continue this for about 5 minutes. Be playful with each other. Get down on the floor and wrestle with each other like cats or dogs would. Put your hands together and push into each other. Do a hand dance. One lead, then the other lead, then flow into each leading spontaneously. Let yourselves be wild and playful and seductive. Be creative with this. The idea is to raise your energy and have strong contact with each other. When you feel complete with this, give each other a full body hug and sit down in front of each other on a meditation cushion or pillows or chairs.

Look into each other's eyes and start breathing through your mouth as if sipping through a straw, bringing your breath from your pelvis to your heart on your inhalation and back down to your pelvis on the exhalation. Begin to harmonize your 2 rhythms until you are breathing together.

Start the pelvic rock. On the exhale, move your pelvis towards your partner. On the inhale, rock your pelvis back away from your partner. This movement combined with breathing opens up the energy channels & begins to create a sexual charge

Start your kegels. On the inhale, tighten your PC muscle and take your sexual energy up the middle of your body from your 1st to 4th chakra. On the exhale, bear down with your PC muscle and bring your sexual energy back down to the 1st chakra.

Creative Play Exercises

Continue the Pelvic Rock & running energy from the 1st to 4th chakra and back down again. On the exhale, send your energy from your heart down to your pelvis and out to your partner's pelvis and up to your partner's heart. On the inhale, bring your energy back from your partner's heart down through his/her genitals to your genitals and up to your heart chakra. Imagine sending love and sexual vitality to your partner, blending your love and sexual pleasure with his/hers and receiving love and sexual intimacy from your partner. Continue this sharing of love and sexual energy until you feel in deep harmony.

Then switch to inverted breathing, As one of you inhales, the other exhales. At the end of the next inhale, Shiva (the man) holds his breath in while Shakti (the woman) continues her breathing by exhaling all of her energy into Shiva's heart center. When Shakti has completed her exhale, Shiva exhales from his heart, through his genitals, up to Shakti's heart as Shakti inhales all of his wonder filled love and sexual energy. Continue pelvic rocking throughout this exercise, one of you rocking forward as the other rocks back, and then reverse the motion.

Shiva and Shakti can now create a complete circle of love and sexual pleasure by Shiva sending his energy from his vajra to his partner's yoni and up to Shakti's heart and from her heart to his heart and from there down to the vajra making a complete circle of love and pleasure. Shakti sends the energy from her heart to Shiva's heart as Shiva inhales. Shiva takes the energy into his heart and then exhales it down & across to Shakti through his vajra.

You can now get into Yab Yum position if you choose to. This position was named by the Buddhists to mean union of mother and father. This is where the woman sits in the man's lap facing him with her arms clasped around him and her legs around his waist. The man has his arms clasped around his Beloved's waist. You can then put your mouths close together. Seal your mouths if you want, one breathing in while the other is breathing out. This creates a closed circuit of energy between Shiva and Shakti and allows them to build their energy higher and higher. Continue this experience until you feel complete and then end when you feel ready. Give each other a full body hug and thank each other for your love and attention.

Then lie together, spoon or find any position that feels good. Share your experience—What felt good? Uncomfortable? What did you learn about yourself? Each other? How do you think this can be used in your relationship or by yourself? What did you learn about the relationship of sexuality, spirituality and love from this experience?

End with bowing to each other, thanking each other and saying namaste to each other.

Exercise 6: Sexual Ecstasy

(Adapted from Margot Anand's Wave of Bliss exercise
as outlined in her book *Art of Sexual Ecstasy*)

Aim:
To teach couples a way of intensifying and merging the energy between them to create a bliss filled and cosmic experience. This also helps couples unite their yin/yang (female–male) energy between them and within them.

Preparation:
Bathe and put on sensual clothing. Allow 45 minutes for this experience. Choose sacred sexual music that is rhythmic yet soothing, romantic and transcendent. Create Sacred Space. Obtain meditation pillows or

several sturdy pillows. Have some scented massage oil and a large towel to protect your pillows from the oil.

Do an opening ritual, meditating for a few minutes with your eyes closed bringing love to yourself and committing to being a vehicle of love for your partner. Open your eyes slowly and see your partner as your precious beloved. Bow to each other, saying namaste, and eye gazing. Share with each other appreciation and love. Share your intention for this process, then any fears you have and the boundaries you have.

Begin to caress each other, including each other's genitals. Make love in whatever way is attractive to you. When you begin to feel sexual arousal, take the Yab Yum position where the man (or 1 partner) is seated on pillows with his legs crossed in meditation position. The woman (or other partner) seats herself on top of the man with her legs behind him and her arms around his back or his neck. This position is the best one for sealing the energy between you and letting it build up. Assume a meditative attitude whenever you are in yab yum position.

Feel free to adapt this position to whatever is comfortable for you where your pelvises are connected and you have access to connect with your hearts and mouths. The idea is not that you have to do this a certain way, but that you are really committed to being close and sharing your energy and your love with each other. Practice going back and forth from the normal positions where you make love to the yab yum position several times. It's important to stay in this position for as long as is comfortable to allow the sexual and love energy to merge and to build.

When you feel ready, move away from each other in a seated position where you are not touching. Take some massage oil, and cover each other's bodies telling each other what you enjoy about each other's bodies, including each other's genitals, so that you are using your touch to bless each other with your appreciation and your love. Stimulate each other's genitals to create more arousal. Resume sacred sexual breathing, breathing from your genitals to your crown chakra on the inhalation and back down to your 1st chakra on the exhalation. Begin pelvic rocking and kegel exercises again to increase your arousal.

Move into Yab Yum position. Women, insert your partner's vajra inside your yoni or right on the outside if there's no erection. Begin alternate breathing where one person breathes out as the other one breathes in. Begin to kiss each other as you do this where you breathe each other's air into your own mouth on the inhale and exhale your own breath into your partner's mouth on the exhalation. When you inhale your partner's breath, send it all the way down to your genitals.

Women, when you exhale and rock your pelvis forward, give your energy, soul and love to your partner through your yoni, into your partner's vajra. Men, as you inhale and rock your pelvis back, you embrace your partner's energy, soul and love with your vajra mingling it with your own, sending it all the way up to your crown center.

Men, when you exhale, send your energy down through your heart to your genitals, and out through your vajra, relaxing your genital muscles as you do this, giving it to your partner who is inhaling and drawing your energy in through her yoni. She mixes your energy with her own and sends it up through her heart and up to her crown.

Continue your mouth-to-mouth breathing. Close your eyes. At the end of breathing out, when you begin your inhale, send pleasure, love, closeness and bliss upwards to transform it through connecting with your third eye and crown chakras. Once you reach the end of your inhalation, hold your breath, keep your genital muscles contracted, and relax the rest of your body. The more you can relax, the more you may experience your energy shooting up towards your 3rd eye and out your crown. At the same time that you have inhaled, your partner has exhaled and has empty lungs. Try to synchronize your breath so you both have several seconds at the end of each inhale and exhale to pause letting the breath shoot up to the crown.

On the exhale, bring the breath back down from your crown to your genitals, imagining white light bathing you on the inside and showering down around you. Continue this breathing until you feel a natural rhythm and relaxation happening where your energies are merging with each other and all of life at the same time. Imagine yourselves as a fountain of light and love offering yourselves, your love and your light to the universe and in turn being blessed by the universe. Feel your oneness with each other and with All That IS.

The final step in this process is to create a continuous, circular flow of energy as it passes up through the woman and down through the man. Shakti starts this by inhaling, drawing her energy from her genitals up to her mouth, not her third eye. Then she exhales into her partner's mouth, sending her energy down through his heart to his sex center, completing one cycle.

On the next inhalation, Shakti again draws energy from her partner's genitals into her own sex center and sends it up through her heart to her mouth. Breathing out, she passes it to Shiva, repeating the cyclical movement of energy.

Shiva imagines the movement of energy in the same way as Shakti. He breathes in the breath, love and energy of his partner through his mouth and sends it all the way down to his genitals. Exhaling, he visualizes the energy passing out through his vajra into his beloved's yoni and then up to her mouth. This creates a closed rhythmic ongoing cycle with relaxed breathing.

Variation of the Closed Circuit Breathing

This helps deepen the couple's feeling of oneness and unity and connection with the cosmos. This is to be done when the above practice has become effortless and natural. You and your partner will be doing visualizations that are different but parallel.

Maintain the alternate breathing. As Shakti inhales, she imagines that she is embracing energy in through her genitals and up her inner channel to her mouth. She exhales, visualizing that she is expressing her energy into her partner's mouth and down through her partner's inner channel to his genitals.

As Shiva inhales, he visualizes that he is drawing energy in through his genitals and up his inner channel to his mouth. He exhales, visualizing that he is sending it into the mouth of his partner and down her inner channel to her genitals, where he begins to pick it up again on his next inhale. Both partners are imagining a continuous cycle of energy, but they are seeing it move in opposite directions. This works fine if each partner continues to focus on his or her own part in this.

This breathing produces a feeling of harmony and deep relaxation, where you become the flow of energy itself, effortless and natural. A balance of opposites begins to occur where you lose a sense of yourself as male or female, human or divine and begin to blend in with the energy of your partner and the energy of the universe. A circle of sacred sexuality is created where the strong energy of your sex center is sent to your crown chakra which then uses it to strengthen the sense of enlightenment and unity with all that is. This energy is then sent back to the sex center to enlighten it through love and oneness with all that is. This is the essence of soulful sex and can transform your lovemaking from ordinary to a sacred, blissful and ecstatic prayer.

When you feel complete with this experience, slow down and be still while remaining inside each other. Stay like this for 5 -10 minutes. To end this, say a prayer of thanksgiving, dedicating this experience to something that both of you value, like world peace or love in everyone's heart or lasting happiness in your own relationship. After completing this, you can move back to normal lovemaking or lie in each other's arms for about 20 minutes without talking.

When you feel ready, discuss what your experience was like for you with one listening while the other talks. What was most pleasureful for you? Ecstatic? What was uncomfortable or difficult? What did you learn about yourself? Your partner? How can you incorporate this practice into your lovemaking repertoire? What step will you take to integrate this into your life together?

Orgasmic Bliss Exercises for Women

The following exercises are based on the premise contained in the book *Sex Matters for Women* by Sally Kope and Dennis Sugrue. They say that " a woman's orgasmic response is learned through experience, experimentation, and self-awareness" (p. 92).

For this reason, I recommend that both women and men take this opportunity to focus in on their own body, their sensations, emotions and desires. It is important to follow every nuance and to take risks to explore and experiment in order to find what feels good. In these exercises, I have used information taken from Margot Anand's 2 videos called Multi Orgasmic Response Ecstasy Training for Men and Their Lovers and for Women and Their Lovers.

I also took some information from Margot's books *Sexual Ecstasy, The Art of Orgasm* and *The Art of Sexual Ecstasy*. These exercises do not go into a detailed description of the different ways of stimulating the clitoris, Graffenberg G-spot, and vajra and prostate. For a complete description of this, go to Margot Anand's books.

Aim:
To teach women and men how to focus totally on their own body and to follow their bliss, In other words, people learn to focus in on their own pleasure and to explore how to build this pleasure by asking their partner to stimulate them and touch them in certain ways that feel right for them.

A second aim is to learn to focus on your own pleasure and stimulation and at the same time to stay connected to and in communication with your partner through eye gazing, being aware of each other's energy and verbal communication. The third aim is to give women an experience of extended sexual pleasure and multiple orgasms.

Preparation:
There is no right or wrong way of doing this, and no particular protocol except to refrain from genital orgasm. Another very important key is for the person receiving the touching and stimulation to be totally tuned into themselves and their sexual response. Be very willing to express verbally to your partner what you are enjoying and what you are not enjoying. If you cannot get your partner to understand how to touch you, take their hand and show them by putting your hand on top of theirs and guiding them as to how to touch you. Be careful about criticism. Don't say you're doing this wrong. Say what you like and then ask them to add or change something.

Creative Play Exercises

We have never really been given permission to tell each other how we like to be touched. We usually worry about being critical or negative so don't say anything. This is your opportunity to really tell your partner what areas you like to be touched in and how you like to be touched. It's also very OK if you don't know what feels great. Feel open to exploring. It's also very normal to want change. Something may feel good one minute, and the next moment, you might want something completely different. Be very willing to explore and be as truthful as possible.

Givers, try to get your ego out of the way. Recognize that your partner's communication to you about your touch is not about you. There is nothing you are doing wrong. Your partner is tuning into his or her own body. No one can know what their body needs at the present moment except them. As much as you think you know your partner, be completely open to serving them and approaching them with beginner's mind, as if you are seeing them and touching them for the first time. Let yourself be totally led by their direction and communication.

If either of you get close to genital orgasm, it's important to stop, breathe, take your energy up to your heart by putting your own hands on your heart or asking your partner to put her/his hands on your heart.

Take any directions for exercises lightly. Do not use this information to set up expectations for yourselves. These directions are simply guidelines for exploring ways of giving yourselves and each other more pleasure. Use these suggestions as jumping off places to experiment with what pleases you. Be your own experts on you. Create a laboratory of safety and pleasure to find out what your particular pleasure patterns are.

Additional Preparation:
Give yourselves about 1 hour apiece for this ritual and processing it with each other. Both of you can shower and dress in something sensual. Shiva can create the sacred space with candles, flowers, and special

sensual music. Have massage oil handy and a sexual lubricant available. Shiva, have pillows for your beloved to elevate her head so she can look at her partner. Shiva can be seated at the side of your partner.

Exercise 1: Pleasuring the Yoni & Clitoris

Do an opening ritual by sharing a Namaste and bow to each other. Share your love and appreciation for each other and your intention, fears and boundaries for this experience.

Shiva can start by putting his hands on his partner's heart, opening his heart to her, looking into her eyes and telling her he loves her and that this is his gift of love to her. He can start synchronizing his breath to hers. Then ask her if he can proceed. When she says yes, he then can use massage oil to start massaging her whole body starting with her feet and legs, putting love into every stroke.

Shiva can really focus on what feels good to himself, putting his heart into his fingertips, using beginner's mind to explore his partner's body as if for the first time. He can see his partner's body as a precious gift she is offering to him. It is up to him to show her how much he appreciates this gift. He can use his hands, his mouth and lips and tongue and breath to please his Beloved. Avoid the clitoris or yoni at first. Use teasing strokes around the genital area and the breasts.Do this for several minutes, massaging every part of her body with love.

Shakti can receive her partner's massage with an open heart, being as receptive to the pleasure of his touch as possible. She can treat his caresses as precious gifts of love from him. She can also be very attentive to what feels good to her and showing and telling her partner with her sounds and body movements and words. This is a special time for Shakti to lead Shiva into giving her more and more pleasure through her very specific and detailed communication about what feels good and what does not. It is important that Shakti be willing to say stop to anything that she does not like. It would help, if she were diplomatic about this, indicating that she would like her Beloved to change what he is doing in a certain way. Remember that this is a very vulnerable time for both of you. Keep making loving eye contact with each other.

In order to heighten her own pleasure, Shakti needs to be doing sexual breathing where she breathes in through her mouth as if sipping into a straw, and breathing out through her mouth. She also can be tightening her PC muscles on her inhalation and releasing them on her exhalation. Pelvic rocking in harmony with her breath is good also as it helps build up the energy in the pelvis. Shakti can be focusing her attention on her first chakra but also on the strokes her partner is giving her, noticing what is pleasing her and what she wants more of.

Shiva can massage the inside of the thighs and continue to tease in and around the yoni and clitoris and breasts to heighten arousal.

Shakti, when you feel filled full with the love and appreciation of your Beloved, and when you feel safe, put some lubricant on your own fingers and begin to stroke your yoni in ways that you like best. This is the time to show your Beloved what kind of touching and stroking you like best. Shiva can back off and watch while Shakti pleasures herself, stroking her yoni, finding just the strokes and touch that are stimulating and arousing.

Shakti, take lots of time to go over your whole yoni, then the outer and inner lips, circling around the inner lips and the mouth of the yoni, telling your Beloved just what feels good, and how to touch you. You can use the description of a clock to describe the areas of your yoni that are most pleasurable, with 12:00 at the top towards your pubic mound and 6:00 at the bottom of your yoni towards your anus. Go to the clitoris. Suzie Heumann suggests "with your thumb and forefinger, feel along both sides of your clitoris. Explore the clitoral shaft buried just under the skin below the clitoris." (*The Everything Great Sex Book* by Suzie Heumann, p. 58). Margot Anand suggests that "you hold the shaft between your thumb and index finger and roll it lightly between them. Experiment until you find this point and then slowly begin to massage evenly, rubbing up and down on either side of the shaft, finding a comfortable rhythm." (*Sexual Ecstasy* by Margot Anand, p. 28). Explore other strokes that feel right to you and attractive to you. As you get more aroused, start lightly touching the tip of the clitoris, still with the hood covering the tip.

Continue this stroke, and as you get more aroused, try pulling back the hood of the clitoris and directly stimulating the tip of the clitoris, rubbing lightly and consistently. This usually can only be pleasurable when Shakti is very aroused, so if it doesn't feel good, don't continue it. Shakti, do not pleasure yourself to full orgasm, but just to a point where you are very aroused. Stay relaxed and receptive to this pleasure. Instead of releasing it, let it spread throughout your entire body.

When you feel you have shown your Beloved just the way to pleasure you best, ask Shiva if he has any questions. He can ask questions all the way through this process so that he really understands how you like to be touched and pleasured. When you are done talking, Shakti can ask Shiva if he would start stroking your yoni.

Shiva, you can take the direction of your Beloved. Follow her lead. If she wants some direction from you, use your own intuition. Go slowly and gently. Start by covering her entire yoni with your hand. Then massage the outside of the lips, then the inner lips and all around the clitoris. Close the lips, then massage the outside of the lips from the bottom up toward the clitoris, then down toward the anus. Do this several times. While you're doing this, Shiva can tease Shakti's clitoris lightly touching around it every once in a while." (*Sexual Ecstasy* by Margot Anand, p. 26). When you think she is ready, ask Shakti if you can touch her clitoris. When she says yes, lightly touch the clitoris. Explore ways of stimulating the clitoris. Work together here. Shakti, give Shiva suggestions about what feels good and what kind of touch is best for you. It's OK if you don't know. Simply use this time to learn.

If you need direction about how to stroke the clitoris, read Margot Anand's book, *Sexual Ecstasy, the Art of Orgasm.* When Shakti is very aroused, you can pull back the hood of the clitoris and directly stimulate the tip of the clitoris rubbing lightly and consistently. If the shaft and tip of the clitoris is stiff and swollen indicating high arousal on Shakti's part, you can " make vertical strokes up and down the sides of the clitoris, or you can pulse, squeezing rapidly or use circular motions". (*Sexual Ecstasy* by Margot Anand, p. 30).

Exercise 2: Pleasuring the G-spot

(Graffenberg or Goddess spot)

Aim:
To identify the goddess spot and to explore stimulating the goddess spot for pleasure and for healing.

Preparation:
You can have another woman initiate you into this practice if you prefer it. If this is the first time you are doing Goddess spot work, I suggest that you do this separately and give it very special attention, as it is a

very vulnerable exercise for most people. If you have done this before, you can add this to the above exercise or do it separately. Take 1 hour for the exercise and processing of feelings. If this is done as a separate exercise, be sure and create sacred space with honoring each other and sharing your desires, fears and boundaries for doing the exercise. If you have fears, look at what the needs are you have that will help you feel safer and share them with each other. If you are new to this exercise, be open to there being some discomfort. Be prepared to breathe through any discomfort, but do not continue if there is any pain. Go at your own pace. Do not push yourself with this. Go as far as you want to and then stop for another day for more work on this. Use a water-based lubricant for inside the yoni like KY jelly or Astroglide.

Shiva, as the giver of love and pleasure, tune into your Beloved with your heart and soul. Give her your full attention and love by putting your hands over her heart and looking into her eyes. Synchronize your breathing with hers.

Begin to massage Shakti all over, finding every spot enjoying her body and her energy, letting her know it and encouraging her to let you know what she likes and what she wants more of or what she wants you to change. Let her be your guide, and her communication with you be your lighthouse. Since Shakti is most receptive to Goddess spot work when she is very aroused, ask her permission to start stimulating her clitoris. If a woman is initiating you and you don't want sexual contact with her, you can stimulate your own clitoris.

Shiva, ask for Shakti's explicit direction so you can give her just the right touch. Know that with most women, their need for certain kinds of stimulation changes moment to moment so you won't know what is next until she tells you. You can explore what works, but use information from her as your ultimate guide.

Creative Play Exercises

When your beloved tells you or shows you that she is very aroused, it is time for stimulation of her G-spot. Ask Shakti's permission to enter her vagina. If she says yes, lubricate your fingers and insert one or two fingers into her vagina with the palm of your hand facing up. Hook your finger pressing up and forward towards the roof of Shakti's yoni. The G-spot is about the size of a nickel and is composed of rough tissue with ridges on it, different from the smooth tissue around it. Explore this area until your Beloved experiences some sensations.

Shakti, be sure to use sexual breathing here, deep and slow to maintain relaxation and to heighten awareness. Shakti can feel it as pleasureful or as particular pressure or an urge to urinate or something that is uncomfortable. There also can be neutral feelings. Maintain eye contact with each other and specific communication about what the sensations are and any feelings or associations. Shakti, talk about anything that is coming up for you, memories, feelings of any kind. No matter if this is the first or 100th time you are doing this work, this area holds tension and there might be areas that are released this time that you may never have experienced before or never will again. Don't try to analyze this. Simply, pay close attention to every detail of sensation.

Shakti, guide Shiva to just the right kind of touch. If you want to be touched in other areas of your yoni besides the g-spot, guide your Beloved to just the spot. Our body holds exquisite wisdom and knows just what it needs if we only listen and follow its guidance.

Shakti, you can explore working with your body and your Beloved's stimulation by moving your hips, rocking your pelvis, breathing strongly and making sounds. Try deep guttural sounds, relaxing your throat and neck or make moans of pleasure. Both of you take time to explore and experiment with what feels good. There might be strong feelings that come up in the form of tears, sobs, anger and screams. Let everything be OK. It's important that both of you understand that the intensity of emotion does not mean that anything is wrong. It's just the release of tension that has been held in our sexual center for a very long time.

Margot Anand suggests some particular strokes for the G-spot work including, "moving in a zigzag pattern crosswise over the whole G-spot area, or pulsating the G-spot with your fingers directly over the area." (See *Sexual Ecstasy* by Margot Anand, p. 55 for other strokes). Shakti needs to open to all the sensations you are experiencing, and expand the sensations through focusing your breath in your pelvis and at your G-spot. Also, imagine that you are giving the sensations space, that you are expanding your boundaries, letting the sensations be there and expand throughout your pelvis and your entire body. Open with love to these sensations like you are welcoming your best friend.

Shakti, you can aid in your own arousal by stimulating your breasts or other parts of your body that want attention. Don't strive for orgasm with this, but if it comes allow it and welcome it. Enhance it with your breathing and maintain eye contact with your Beloved in this process. If this is your first experience with this, continue to simply expand the pleasure with your breathing. If you have done this before, explore shooting your energy up to your heart and to your third eye and your crown center when you are highly aroused or when you are at the point of orgasm. Notice what happens and how doing this affects your experience.

When Shakti feels complete, tell Shiva and thank him generously for his help and support. Lie in each other's arms and talk about your experience with each other. Tell each other what you liked, what kind of pleasure you felt, what if any tension or discomfort you might have experienced, how you felt about your communication, what you liked about the support from each other, what you would have liked to be different. What did you learn from this experience about yourself and about your partner? Close your session with bowing to each other and saying Namaste and thanking God/Goddess, Source of All That is for this experience and dedicating the fruits of your experience to your own healing and to world peace.

Exercise 3: Blended Orgasm

Aim:

To facilitate Shakti receiving G-spot and clitoral stimulation that can enable her to experience orgasmic pleasure for a prolonged period of time.

Preparation:

If you want specific strokes for creating a blended orgasm, consult Margot Anand's book, *Sexual Ecstasy*. If this is the first time you have tried this, do this exercise by itself. If you have done the clitoral and G-spot stimulation exercises before, you can try this as a part of the 2 exercises described above. Be sure you are rested enough to do this. Take about 1 hour for this by itself, including the processing. Shiva, prepare a sacred space. Bathe and dress in your sexiest clothing. Shiva, treat your Beloved as your Queen and escort her to your sacred space, as if it is the most beautiful love palace in the world, created for just the 2 of you, a magical and mystical place within which you can be totally safe and creative, communicative and loving.

Shiva, help your Beloved to become very comfortable with pillows propping her head up so that she can see you and a towel underneath her to protect any beautiful sheets you might have arranged. Be sure you are comfortable in a position that you can access stimulating Shakti's G-spot and clitoris.

When you are both ready, Shiva, you can begin by placing your hand on Shakti's heart, telling her you love her and asking for her permission and direction to give her as much pleasure as possible. Share your desires, fears and boundaries for doing this exercise. Maintain eye contact as you share together. Shiva, start massaging Shakti all over lovingly and gently at first. Synchronize your breath with Shakti. Shakti, open yourself up to Shiva's attention and respond with your own love and receptivity.

When your beloved is ready, ask permission to touch and stimulate her yoni and her clitoris. When you feel her arousal is high, ask to come inside her with your fingers. Begin G-spot stimulation. Establish a rhythm of stimulation of the G-spot and clitoris at the same time or alternate between the two, based on Shakti's preference. Shakti, communicate with your Beloved about what feels good and what you want more of or different. Shiva, use your creativity and intuition and knowledge to explore pleasuring your Beloved in just the way that feels good. Remember that this is a learning exercise and you are taking directions from Shakti. Shiva, you can't be the expert on Shakti. She needs to give you directions about how to please her.

Shakti, when you have found the right combination of strokes that are bringing you more arousal, let Shiva know so he can continue this for a longer time. Again, don't be afraid to ask for change if you need it. Shiva, the more intense Shakti's excitement becomes, the more regular your strokes need to be. When Shakti is approaching orgasm, slow down, tease her, keep helping her build her arousal, bringing her several times to a peak without going over the edge.

Shakti, keep relaxing, letting your pleasure and excitement build and ripple out to all parts of your body. Remember to use your breath, movement including pelvic rocking and kegels, and sound to intensify your arousal. Shakti, do not hold your breath at this point.

Keep breathing deeply and rapidly. It is fine to keep experiencing waves of pleasure.

Shakti, if your arousal builds to a peak after several times of coming to the edge of orgasmic pleasure, let yourself have an orgasm. Don't try for it, but let it happen. Keep your eyes open and let the energy of your orgasm shoot out to your partner. Also, send your energy up to your heart and to your 3rd eye and crown center. Shiva, keep your hands in place, though not moving while your Beloved is having her orgasm, so that you are ready to facilitate her expanding her pleasure.

Shiva, once Shakti's first orgasmic peak has passed, start to stimulate areas of Shakti's body that are ready for it and open to it. It is OK to ask to rest and bathe in the pleasure you already have. This resting actually works to enhance your pleasure. When you are ready, Shakti, tell your Beloved and let yourself open to more stimulation. Keep breathing and re-circulating your energy, taking the intense pleasure up to your heart and your crown chakra. Keep doing kegels and pelvic rocking.

Connect your heart center with your partner's. Synchronize your breathing again. Shakti, let your body stream energy and open to any way that your body is expressing including shaking or spasms. Let yourself moan or scream or cry or simply feel in every way. Welcome all of the different ways your body is experiencing and expressing pleasure. Do not shut down or stop breathing or turn off. If you feel yourself doing this, bring yourself back to the present moment. So often, at this point, it is very easy to stop.

Let yourself explore receiving more and more pleasure, expanding your boundaries to create more and more space and include more and more pleasure. Give your Beloved direction about where and how you want to be stimulated in your clitoris, G-spot or anywhere else. Both of you can imagine that Shakti's pleasure is a fountain of love that is bathing both of you in Blessing from the Universe. This is a very ecstatic state and can be timeless. Let yourselves continue this for as long as your would like.

When Shakti feels complete and satiated, tell your Beloved. Thank him for all the pleasure that you have experienced. Both of you can say a prayer of thanksgiving to your bodies and to your spirit guides for all of the wonder filled experiences you have had. You can then dedicate your experience for your own healing and for world peace. Once you have completed this, lie in each other's arms and process this experience. What was the high point for each of you? What was the low point or times that you might have been confused or out of touch with each other. What did you learn about yourself and each other through this practice? Is there any of this that you would like to incorporate into your regular lovemaking experiences? If so, what would that be? Is there any healing that happened during this experience for either of you? If so, what? After processing this, complete this experience by giving each other a hug, bowing and saying Namaste to each other.

Margot Anand reports that "experiencing blended orgasms....enhances the production of endorphins, making people more relaxed, healthy, and happy, reducing tension and stress" (*The Art of Sexual Ecstasy* by Margot Anand, p. 66)

Creative Play Exercises

Orgasmic Bliss Exercises for Men

Exercise 1: Pleasuring the Penis & Lasting Longer

Aim:
To help men last longer, have more pleasure and experience multiple orgasms and blended orgasms (through stimulation of the penis and prostate).

Preparation:
In this exercise men need to know how to stop their urge to ejaculate. There are several very effective techniques to do this. The first one is taking his own hand to his heart or having his partner put her hand on his heart and spread the energy from his vajra to his heart and throughout his body to his crown chakra. Other exercises are:

1. Stop the Stimulation. The man pays attention to when he is starting to lose control of his urge to ejaculate. His partner and he agree on a specific word or signal ahead of time to use when he gets to this point, like stop or slow down, or a hand signal, like putting up one hand. The man expresses the word or signal and he and his partner stop all stimulation and lay in each other's arms talking, eye gazing and simply resting together until he feels his stimulation has gone down. Then start lovemaking again.

2. Kegels. A man can contract his PC muscle and hold it to the count of 10 and then release it. This can take away the urge to ejaculate.

3. Pressing deeply on the perineum, the area between the penis and the anus at the onset of orgasm. This area accesses the prostate and can prevent ejaculation and prolong orgasmic pleasure.

4. Squeeze Technique—When the man feels the urge to ejaculate, he can squeeze the shaft of the penis, where the shaft meets the head, with the thumb on the top and the forefinger and middle finger on the underside.

Both partners need to shower and dress sensuously. Have sexual lubrication and organic massage oil available.

Shakti, create a beautiful sacred space for your Beloved. Lead him to your space as if he is your king and you are being a queen to him, lavishing him with love and attention. Be sure there are pillows for his comfort and a towel beneath him to protect any sheets from oil and body fluids. Seat yourself between his legs close to his vajra. You can sit cross-legged on pillows and put his legs over your knees. Feel free to change positions to find just what is right for you.

Share your desires fears and boundaries. Shiva, this is your time to be totally receptive, taking in Shakti's attention and love. This may be a vulnerable and uncomfortable time for you. Many men don't know what their needs are because they don't focus on them. They are rarely in the role of receiver, especially physically. Give yourself time to learn what you need and what feels good. Be willing to communicate consistently with your Beloved and tell her as best as you can what feels good. This is very important for her to know how to proceed.

Both of you need to stay away from goals and expectations. This is not about achieving anything, It is about learning to give and receive pleasure in the moment and follow the responses of the body.

Creative Play Exercises

Begin with a long full-body hug, melting into each other's arms, opening your heart to each other. Shakti can put your hand on Shiva's heart and send him love. Shakti, you can look into Shiva's eyes and share how much you love him and want to please him and give him the most pleasurable experience possible. Synchronize your breathing with him. Put massage oil on your hands and start with his feet, massaging his whole body, pouring your love and support into your touch. Focus on yourself and your own pleasure when you do this massage. This will be a way of being fully present to Shiva. Do not talk much. Shiva, do sexual breathing, kegels, pelvic rocking and other movements and sounds to enhance your pleasure. Let yourself be a sponge and soak up the pleasure.

Let Shakti know what you enjoy with your sounds, moans and groans and by your words. If you want Shakti to do something specific, tell her or show her by putting your hand over hers and guiding her to the stroke that is right for you. Shakti, you can go to Shiva's genital area and massage his pelvis and penis and testicles. You can take his testicles in your hands and cup your hands to hold his balls. Gently massage his testicles and play with his penis. Ask him if you can now massage his penis. Put lots of lubrication on your hands and keep his penis very lubricated. Explore different strokes, using your own creativity and intuition, and following your own pleasure as well as his direction. Use his penis as your plaything. You might try stroking his whole vajra from top to bottom and bottom to top. You might try stroking from the base up to the top, continuously. Another stroke would be to take both hands and stroke from the bottom to the top and then to reverse and go from the top to the bottom. Something else to try would be to take your hands one at a time in circular motions around his vajra. Caress his testicles and stimulate his perineum between his testicles and his anus. This area can take strong pressure. Palpate this area and ask for direction as to what feels especially good. You can use your lips and mouth and tongue and hair and face and breasts to stimulate him. Try for what's new as well as what is familiar and well known to please him. Shiva, keep giving Shakti feedback on what feels good. Don't trance out. Try to maintain eye contact with her and tell her with moans or words what feels good. Shakti, keep asking for feedback.

Shakti, build arousal in Shiva by increasing the pace and rhythm of your stroking. Tease Shiva by varying the pressure, lightly tickling the head and the frenulum (the sensitive indentation of the underside of the penis where the shaft meets the ridge), then holding the base of Shiva's vajra with one hand, and with the other hand, grasping the shaft, and stroking the shaft firmly up and down.

If the penis seems to lose responsiveness or become numb, stop the stimulation here and start massaging Shiva's whole body, kissing and teasing. Find other ways of pleasing Shiva. When it feels right, go back to caressing Shiva's vajra and find just the strokes that feel best and increase the intensity of your stimulation. Shiva can pay close attention to the sensations in your Vajra. Increase the rapidity and strength of your breath, and do kegels and pelvic rocking. Move your body to enhance Shakti's strokes. Shiva, when you feel that you are close to orgasm and ejaculation, say stop and discontinue all stimulation to the penis. Shiva can contract his PC muscles. Shakti can press strongly into Shiva's perineum point with your index and middle finger of one hand, while holding Vajra with the other. This will stop the urge to ejaculate. If you need more control, Shakti can press firmly with the thumbs and fingers of both hands on the vajra shaft just below the head.

Shakti can take her hand to Shiva's heart and spread his energy throughout his chest and up to his third eye and top of his head. Shiva can continue to relax and let go, letting the sensations spread throughout his entire body, enjoying the sensations without trying to make anything happen or go towards the goal of orgasm and ejaculation. When Shiva feels ready, Shakti can start the stimulation again.

Over the next half-hour, Shakti can bring Shiva to the point of ejaculation 3-6 times, stopping to relax and then re-stimulate. At the end of this time, if Shiva wants to come to a climax, allow this to happen. Shiva can maintain eye contact with Shakti during his orgasm shooting his love out his eyes and his heart to his Beloved. He can then direct his energy up to his heart and to his third eye and his crown center to explore a cosmic orgasm. It would be good for him to continue to expand his energy to keep opening up to more pleasure even at this point of orgasm.

Shiva, let the energy flow and vibrations and streaming happen. Again, don't be afraid of the intensity of pleasure. Enjoy it and embrace it. When you feel complete, lie in Shakti's arms and express gratitude to her for her giving and loving. You can say a prayer of thanksgiving to God and all of Life for this grand experience. Dedicate your loving to your own healing and to peace on the planet. When you feel complete, share what your process was. What was the high point for each of you? Were there times, you felt you lost contact with each other. Do either of you have any questions for the other about this process? What did you learn? What do you want to incorporate into your regular lovemaking routine? Close with a full-body hug and Namaste and bow to each other.

Exercise 2: Pleasuring the Prostate

Aim:
To give a man 2 different ways of pleasuring the prostate and to give him an experience of receptivity and vulnerability (connecting to his feminine side). To help a man learn more about his body including the

possibility of an anal massage and what he needs to feel pleasure.
To help a man learn how to expand his capacity to hold pleasure and to intensify it.

Preparation:
If you want to learn specific strokes for massaging the penis and prostate, read Margot Anand's book, *Sexual Ecstasy*.

Take about 45 minutes for this exercise alone. Have oil based lubricant for the external massage and water based lubricant for the inner massage. Shower and dress sensuously. Have latex gloves available for the anal massage. Shiva, be sure to have voided your bladder and rectum. Shakti, arrange the sacred space with all the things your beloved likes. Shakti, cultivate an attitude of gifting your man with the precious treasure of your body and your wisdom as a Goddess of pleasure. Know that he is very vulnerable in this space of receptivity so be open to nurturing him in your very special Goddess way and initiating him into the mystery of the feminine (the receptive mode that you naturally know by your very nature).

Shiva, let go of your need to control this situation. Open to learning about your own body and being willing to receive pleasure. Cultivate an attitude of listening to your body and communicating your sensations and desires to your partner. Imagine that you are simply a vehicle for communication from your body to your partner for the purpose of pleasure. Imagine receiving the gift of her energy and her touch for your enjoyment and learning. See her as the Goddess of Love and Pleasure sent to you by the Universe to teach you about loving yourself, her and Life. Shakti, invite Shiva to take a position lying on his back with pillows underneath his head. You can position yourself between his legs close to his vajra. Both of you bow to each other and say Namaste and share your desires, fears and boundaries for this experience.

Exercise 3: *Massage of the Body & Perineum*

Shakti, you can start by placing your hand on your Beloved's heart, looking into his eyes and synchronizing your breathing with his and sharing what's in your heart. You might tell him how much you love him and how much you want to bless him with your touch. Lubricate your hands with massage oil. Start massaging him from his feet up covering every part of his body sending your love through your hands. Realize what a powerful skill you have to send your Beloved your love for his healing and health.

Then, ask Shiva to roll over onto his stomach and massage the back of his legs especially his upper thighs, buttocks and the small of his back. At the end of this, use a chopping motion to massage his buttocks. Then roll his hips from side to side encouraging him to relax and let go and breathe deeply. This will help prepare him for work on his prostate.

After allowing your Beloved to lie still soaking up the pleasure of the massage, turn him over and start massaging the upper thighs and pelvic area and belly and chest. Ask Shiva's permission to start pleasuring his penis. Put lots of lubrication onto your hands and move into the pubic area and start massaging the testicles and penis. Be creative and playful with your strokes. Shiva, let Shakti know what feels good with your words and your sounds and your movements. Shiva, do sexual breathing and kegels and pelvic rocking to build pleasure and arousal.

Shakti you can use every part of your body even your vulva and clitoris to please your beloved. You can also use your breath blowing into his ear and on his neck and you can use words. Tease him. Seduce him. Know your powers

as a woman to take him higher and higher into ecstasy and pleasure.
Shiva, pay attention to your level of arousal. Allow yourself to come higher and higher to the point just before ejaculation. Then use your stop signal. Shakti, stop all stimulation. Take your hand to Shiva's heart and spread his energy up to his heart.

Shiva, let the energy disperse throughout your body. You can help yourself stop your urge to ejaculate through doing kegels. Contract your PC muscles strongly. If Shiva needs more help, Shakti can press the lower fleshy part of her palm against his perineum, the area between his testicles and his anus.

After the two of you have rested, Shakti can start to re-stimulate Shiva and start the process of arousal again. Use this approach until you bring Shiva to the point of ejaculation several times and you observe that he is highly aroused. This is the point that you can start massaging his prostate from his perineum. Explore this area by caressing, rubbing, pressing and palpating this area or vibrating the area with your thumbs or palms. Shiva, give your beloved direction about what feels good and what you want more of or less of. Be vocal about this.

Exercise 4: Stimulating the Perineum & Prostate

After you have explored pleasuring the perineum, Shakti can add stimulation of the Vajra. Begin by lubricating the vajra with massage oil and start using your favorite strokes to arouse Shiva. Add stimulation to the perineum with your free hand. Press, rub, palpate or vibrate or use circular motions to stimulate the perineum. Find a rhythm that you can use for both the penis and the perineum at the same time.

Shiva, give your Beloved feedback about what feels good: where the best places on your penis and your perineum are to stimulate, what rhythm and pace of pleasuring feels best. Keep eye contact with your Beloved. Make this a couple experience instead of just a solo inward experience. If you want to, you can take this stimulation to a peak where your man is almost ready to orgasm. At this point, your Beloved can say stop and all stimulation ceases. Shiva can really open to the ecstatic sensations in his penis and perineum spreading them throughout his entire body. Open to these sensations and allow them to pleasure you intensely. Allow vibrations (streaming) to flow throughout your entire body.

After resting awhile, Shakti can start the re-stimulation process again. Do this to the point of orgasm several times. If you have done this at least 3 times and Shiva wants to have an orgasm, then allow yourself to go there. At the point of orgasm, keep your eyes open and send love to your partner through your heart and your eyes as well as your body. Also, shoot your energy up to your crown chakra and out the top of your head, connecting with the cosmos. Feel your oneness with yourself, your partner, and with all of Life.

Lie in each other's arms awhile until Shiva feels complete. Dedicate your loving and pleasure to your own healing and the healing of all couples and relationships on the planet. Process your experience with each other. Tell each other what you enjoyed, what you felt confused about or uncomfortable about, what you might want to change next time, what you learned about yourself and your partner, what you would like to incorporate into your regular lovemaking. Thank each other and complete this experience with a full-body hug and a namaste.

Soulful Sex

Exercise 5: Anal & Prostate Massage & Stimulation

(Adapted from *The Art of Sexual Ecstasy* by Margot Anand)

Aim:

To introduce men to an experience of receptivity, of connecting to the yin or feminine side of themselves.

To help men identify the prostate from the inside of the anus and to learn to massage this area for pleasure and for health.

To give men an opportunity to explore the sensations of pleasure in the anus and the prostate and to release tension that might have accumulated over time in the anus and prostate.

To give men an opportunity to experience a deep and powerful internal orgasm.

Preparation:

If this is an add-on exercise, take this time to freshen up. If you're beginning with this exercise, be sure you have both showered and put your most sensual clothing on. Shakti, create sacred space. Give about 1 hour for this exercise. Have water based lubrication for this experience. Shakti, have latex gloves if you prefer this. Be sure your finger nails on the fingers you will use to penetrate your Beloved's anus are cut and filed smoothly.

Start by sitting in front of each other, bowing and saying Namaste. Then share your desires, fears and boundaries for this experience. This experience is loaded with negative messages from society and possibly

Creative Play Exercises

from your early history. There might be history of sexual abuse or shameful experiences that you have had from parents or friends in regard to your anus and your sexuality. This is a very delicate and sensitive area, so talk about any inhibitions, fears, shame, guilt, worry or confusion that you might have. Ask for support by setting boundaries, what you would like to ask your partner to do and not to do. Give each other a hug and move into a position where Shiva has his head on pillows so he can see and maintain eye contact with Shakti. Shakti, position yourself between Shiva's legs so you are close to the prostate and vajra.

Shakti, lubricate your hands with massage oil, and then place your hand over Shiva's heart and look into his eyes, telling him how much you love him and want to give to him for his highest good and pleasure. Send your love to him through your eyes and hands and heart. Shiva, thank your beloved for being here and offering this gift of touch and healing to you. Tell her that you are open to receive her. Both of you synchronize your breathing with each other.

Shiva, begin sexual breathing and kegels where you contract your PC muscle on the inhale and release and bear down on the exhale sending your energy and your breath into your genitals. Do pelvic rocking to harmonize with your kegels and breath. Shakti, massage Shiva all over from his feet up to his inner thighs, and up to his belly, chest neck and face.

With his permission, start stroking his vajra, as he needs to be very aroused to do the prostate massage. Use all your body to stimulate his penis. Do your own sexual breathing and synchronize your breathing with Shiva's. Imagine his penis and his body is your sexual plaything and that the two of you have a wonderful opportunity to play together and give each other much pleasure and joy. Shakti, use your intuition as well as all the wisdom you've gained from your experiences with your Beloved to please him in just the way you like and he likes. Shiva, remember that Shakti needs your direction. Listen to your own body and share what pleases you and what more you want your Beloved to do to please you even more. Shiva, continue to breathe deeply and send your energy down to your genitals.

Shakti, when Shiva is very aroused, put your latex gloves on your non-dominant hand, lubricate your fingers with water based lubricant, and lubricate Shiva's anus and perineum. Begin to slowly massage and caress the anus, using gentle sensitive strokes and letting yourself be guided by Shiva's communication about what feels good and arousing. Shiva, be open to exploring your sensations. Let Shakti know if it's neutral or positive. If anything feels negative or painful, ask for a change. Shiva, keep doing kegels and on your exhalation, bear down strongly sending your breath and energy into your pelvis and anus, letting yourself feel all the sensations and heighten them through your breath. Shakti, continue to stimulate Shiva's lingam (penis) during this process.

Shakti, when you feel Shiva is ready for your penetration into his anus, ask his permission to enter. When he says yes, start with your longest finger with your palm up to enter his anus slowly and gently. Shiva, you can contract your PC muscles which will draw Shakti's fingers into you. At the same time, it's important to relax and let go. If you feel yourself getting tense, just relax. Shakti, if you feel any physical resistance as you enter the anus, just pause and wait until the resistance passes, breathing with Shiva, reminding him to breathe deeply, relax, let go and contract his PC muscles to bring you even further into his anus. Shakti, continue to enter his anus until your finger is about 1 inch inside and then move your finger all around the anus to explore the territory. Shiva, guide her with your words as to what feels good or neutral and how the pace is. Continue sexual breathing. Find areas that are particularly pleasureful and stay there, experimenting with strokes like pressing or vibrating or rubbing back and forth over an area.

Shakti, when you feel Shiva is relaxing into your touch, move your finger a little deeper and curve it up slightly, and feel for the prostate which is described by Margot Anand as a "round firm body of tissue that is shaped like a chestnut." (*Sexual Ecstasy*, p. 128). Suzie Heumann describes it in her book as "like a large soft life-saver, with a slight, soft indention in the center and a round firm but pliable structure". (*The Everything Great Sex Book*, p. 209). Explore stimulating this area by rubbing all around it and over it. Palpate it and vibrate it, press into it firmly, zigzag back and forth over the area, and rim around it. Explore the area all around it. Shakti, look for Shiva's direction with this.

Continue stimulation of the vajra as you are stimulating the prostate. Heighten the stimulation till you approach orgasm, then back away with stopping or lessening the stimulation. Shakti can keep her finger pressed against the prostate, which will also lessen the urge to ejaculate. After resting, re-stimulate to build pleasure. When you reach an orgasmic peak, Shiva can totally relax letting the orgasmic sensations spread into your whole body. Shiva you can allow the streaming vibrations of orgasmic bliss to happen throughout your entire being. Enhance this with deep slow breathing. Take your energy and your focus to your crown center so you can experience a cosmic orgasm.

You can repeat this again and again, intensifying your pleasure with each orgasmic peak you reach. Allow yourself to relax into it and enhance it with your breath and with your attention. This streaming of energy can last a long time, and won't necessarily stop when you stop this exercise. You are creating a template of pleasure for yourself. Now that your body knows what's possible, it will be easier to come here again and again, creating more lasting pleasure for you more and more often in your lovemaking and in your life.

Shiva, when you feel complete, you can tell Shakti. She can stop her stimulation of you and both of you can lie in each other's arms, harmonize your breathing and enjoy the orgasmic ecstatic experience you have created. As you are ready, you can process this experience, letting each other know what your high and low points were, what you learned, what you would like to change next time and what you would like to incorporate into your everyday lovemaking.

Be patient with this exercise. It may take time for Shiva to develop comfort and sensations that are pleasureful with this experience. Or Shiva may decide he does not want to continue exploring this option for pleasure. Be open to what works and what feels best for both of you. If you didn't gain anything else from this experience, the massage of the anus will release much tension that may have been held inside for a long time. The more tension we can release from our bodies, the less armoring we have physically and the more we free ourselves up for higher and higher consciousness.

When you both feel ready to end, thank each other for this experience, dedicate your pleasure to your own healing and to world peace, give each other a full body hug and end with Namaste.

Weaving Sex, Love & Spirit into Everyday Life

Hopefully, the exercises that I have offered you up to the present time have helped you develop skill in expressing your sexuality, opening to Spirit, and acting in more loving ways. The question addressed here is how to live in a loving way everyday. The following exercises are offered to help you do this.

Creative Play Exercises

Exercise 1: Developing Your Purpose for Living

The following exercise drawn from the work of Arnold Patent in the book *You Can Have It All* helps people find meaning in their lives. Often, people ask questions like: What does my life mean? What is important about living? Why try to act in responsible or loving ways? How can I contribute to life? What does sex have to do with all of this?

Having a purpose statement can make everything you do meaningful and worthwhile. It can also give direction to your choices. It provides a way of evaluating everything you do according to the larger picture of what is most important to you.

The following exercise has three steps. Answer the questions, then put it all together.

1a. Name 3 of the qualities that you like best about yourself such as enthusiasm, caring, strong minded.

1b. Name 3 ways you like to interact in the world such as talking and listening, dancing, helping others

1c. Name your ideal world. If you could design the world just the way you ideally would like it, how would it be? An example is a world where everyone is treated in loving ways and where there is abundance for all especially the children.

1d. Put the 3 parts together in a purpose statement. An example is: My purpose is to use my enthusiasm, caring and strong minded nature to talk and listen to others, help them and spread my joy for living through dancing to create a world where everyone is loved and where there is abundance and peace for all especially the children.

1e. Notice how you feel when you say this. If it makes you happy or feels right to you, use it. If it doesn't, continue to refine it until it fits you. Try to make your purpose statement into 1 sentence that really fits you and that you can remember and repeat from memory. The above purpose statement could be made more precise in the following way. My purpose is to enthusiastically serve others and to co-create a loving, peaceful and abundant world.

A final way of testing how well your purpose statement fits you is to say it to several people who know you well. Their feedback can help you refine it even further so it fits you like a glove.

Exercise 2: Creating a Vision Statement to Help You Live Your Purpose

A vision statement helps you make your purpose concrete in your everyday life. It is composed of specific actions and details of living that reflect what is most important to you. It acts as a beacon that guides you towards what you value and believe in as you live your life.

The following exercise is taken from the *Relationship Success Training for Singles Manual* by David Steele & Marvin Cohen. Read through the directions below for the guided visualization, then go into meditation and let your inner wisdom be your guide as to what to focus on.

Sit quietly for 20 minutes in a meditation posture, with your back straight on a meditation cushion or in a chair or lying down on your back. Focus on your breathing, and deepen it and slow it down. Concentrate on your breath and whatever is most prominent about your breathing. Slowly let yourself relax by letting go of any tension on the exhalation and breathing in peace on the inhalation. Remember a time you were filled with love. It could be a time when you were with someone who loves you deeply or a time when you were in nature or with a wonderful pet. When you feel yourself filled with the light of love and when you feel very relaxed, imagine that you are going into a room labeled My Ideal Life. Notice what the doorway to this room looks like. Then notice the door itself. Now, open the door and go into the room and look around. Notice what you see. Investigate everything. Notice colors, the size of the room, the objects in the room. Notice if there are people in the room and who they are. Interview any people who are there finding out as much about them as you can. Let yourself examine everything very closely, noticing all the details. You might also notice if there are any windows in the room, and what the outside of the room looks like that might be connected to your ideal life.

After you have fully examined everything in the room, let your mind open further to any other images of your ideal life, as you would enjoy it most. Imagine yourself with the kind of body you want, the health you want, the ideal way you look, the way you act, the way you feel. Notice what you are thinking about, what your values are, what your lifestyle is in your ideal life. Notice where you live geographically and what kind of house you live in. Be as detailed as possible. Notice who you are associating with. Notice who your ideal partner is and how the two of you are interacting. Notice the overall relationship you have with this person and also what your ideal sexual relationship is like. Notice who your friends are, what your relationships with your family are like. Notice what kind of work you do, how much money you make, what your hobbies are and what your interests are. Notice how you express your spirituality, and how you express your love to yourself and others.

Notice what you enjoy and how you use your time. Again, be as detailed as possible.

When you are done with your meditation, draw or color or paint what you experienced in your guided visualization. You can also do a collage if you wish to express your experience in another way.

When you have finished your creation, look at it and write as if you are the picture expressing yourself. Start with I am... and then let the words flow to describe the picture in the first person. An example would be "I am healthy and happy and vibrantly alive. I am in love with life, with my partner and with all my friends and family. I spread joy through sharing special times with those that I love. I live in a light filled home, on the edge of a beautiful big blue lake that is warm and inviting to swim in."

When you are done with your creative picture and with the writing, write your vision statement. Start with an I am statement to describe your ideal self, your health, and your ideal mental and emotional and spiritual states. An example would be: I am a beautiful vibrantly healthy and alive woman who is upbeat positive, creative and loving.

Then with 1 or 2 sentences each, describe your ideal relationship, your ideal family life, your ideal place you live and your ideal work experience and the ideal way you have fun and the way you express your spirituality. An example would be: My partner and I love each other passionately and treat each other kindly and respectfully. We love playing in bed and in nature. We live in a light filled home by a beautiful lake in a warm and sunny environment. We work together doing retreats in beautiful places and coaching couples and individuals in tantra. We have much fun hiking, swimming, boating and generally being in the outdoors. We pray many times every day, thanking our creator for all the wonder filled ways we have been blessed.

When you have developed your vision statement, type it clearly and neatly and put it in a place where you can look at it and read it every day. Take time when you are feeling comfortable, relaxed and good, and read the vision statement and imagine yourself living your ideal life, feeling the feelings of being in your ideal state. It is important you visualize this when you are feeling good. You don't necessarily have to be feeling good about the ideal life you want to create, but just feeling good in general will help you attract more of what you want. Remember, if you can think it, you can create it. Start now.

Exercise 3: The Wheel of Life

Go to the Wheel of Life diagram (p. 171 of the book *Soulful Sex*). Rate the current level you are at in each area, 10 being the ideal way you want to be, and 0 being no participation or success. Put a line through each section to indicate the level you are at. When you have completed this, then go back and prioritize which 3 areas are most important to you. With each of these 3 areas, jot down several actions you will do to improve your success rate. Put a time line as to when you will complete these steps. Set a time when you will re-evaluate how you have done in following through. Schedule the re-evaluation time on your calendar so that you will be reminded to revisit this plan to see how you are doing. During the re-evaluation session, go back over the 3 highest priorities and measure the growth rate you have developed. Redefine your goals and set some new deadlines for yourself.

You can use this wheel of life to do goal setting and action planning regularly. If there are areas that you especially want to focus on that are not on the wheel, add them. You might rate your sexual relationship and set some goals for improving this area.

Soulful Sex

Exercise 4: Loving Prayers

First thing in the morning, as you awaken from sleep, thank God/ Goddess, Source of All That Is for another day of loving Her, loving yourself and loving life itself. Say your name to yourself, and the words I love you. Ask yourself what 1 loving thing you would like to do for yourself today and then make a plan to do it. Ask yourself what your intention is for the day and how you will meet it.

As the day progresses, ask yourself frequently, what is the loving thing to do in this situation? With every person you meet, see them as your beloved and show them love as much as you can.

With every situation, notice how open, vulnerable and loving you are. If you are not, ask yourself, how did you block yourself from being loving. What do you need to feel safe enough to open up and love? What will you do to meet your own need? Recognize that life itself is your primary partner and that you need to show up as your ideal loving partner. If you are not doing this, ask yourself, how you are blocking yourself and how will you change. If life doesn't go your way, get in the habit of asking yourself what you can learn from this situation. We don't always have control over what life gives us, but we can choose how we will relate to what we're given. We can choose to open up and love or close down and remain stagnant. It's our choice.

Set up rituals where you can remember to pray and give thanks. Meals are a wonderful time to do this. Meditate on the food before you. Enjoy the sight of the food and the smell. Bless the food and give thanks for the food and all the people who brought the food to your table. Give thanks for all the abundance in your life and for your relationships with those that you love. Eat consciously, enjoying the taste of the food, eating slowly and savoring every bite. If you are in a relationship, use meal times as a sacred way of getting to know one another. You might focus on a particular theme for conversation. Be conscious about how you want to use this time together.

At the end of the day, ask yourself how you did in loving yourself and others and meeting your intention for the day. Find one thing that you did that was loving and thank yourself for doing this. Forgive yourself and others for what didn't go well. Go to sleep focusing on what you are grateful for. If you are in a relationship, as you drift off to sleep, share what you are grateful for in each other and your relationship. Remember that the first thoughts you have in the morning and the last thoughts you have in the evening are very powerful. Be conscious of setting your mind up to think positively by focusing on the positive the first and last thing every day.

Exercise 5: Energetic Connections

Tantra is about moving energy and connecting energetically. Energetic connections are powerful ways of harmonizing and blending energy that build intimacy and deepen love and harmony between people.

The first thing in the morning and the last thing at night, spoon together and harmonize your breathing, where you breathe together as one. Do this for 5-10 minutes. The man can also enter the woman even if his penis is soft. He can then simply rest quietly and breathe together.

A melting hug either standing or lying together can also be very harmonizing energetically. This can be done to resolve conflict or to build closeness. Stand or lie face to face. Move into each other's bodies so that your arms are around each other and each part of your body is touching each other. Stay in this position for 3-5 minutes breathing together and feeling into each other. Notice yourself and any way you may be holding back. Let yourself surrender into the other, melting any boundaries and merging with your partner. Deliberately open your heart and let your heart connect with your partner. Notice how you feel after doing this. Share your feelings with your partner.

Eye gazing, putting your hands on each other's hearts while sending love to each other through your hands and harmonizing your breathing are very powerful ways of feeling close to each other. Do this while standing or lying together. When you look into each other's eyes, keep your gaze soft and open taking in your partner's entire face. Stay relaxed and imagine bringing your partner into your heart with your eyes on the inhalation. Send your love out to your partner through your eyes on the exhalation. Do this for at least 5 minutes. Notice how you feel after you do this. Share your feelings with your partner. Sometimes, it takes time to learn to be comfortable with this exercise. Be willing to continue to practice this until if feels comfortable and loving and intimate.

You might do this practice regularly at least once a week to deepen intimacy or maybe more frequently. This can also be done when there is conflict as a way of resolving the differences or healing hurt.

Exercise 6: Expanding Sexuality with Erotic Surprises

This exercise is designed to spice up your sex life by finding out just what your partner likes and giving it to him/her. If you are single, do this individually and then create an erotic surprise for yourself regularly.

Creative Play Exercises

Each person needs to make a list of the erotic experiences that are turn ons for him or her. Be wild and creative about this. The sky is the limit. Be as far out and yet as honest as possible. Some turn ons might be making love in the forest, coming home to your partner wearing nothing but some jewelry, enjoying a hot bubble bath together, receiving a sensual massage from your beloved, etc.

Once you have made your lists, exchange them and discuss them. Read your lists out loud to each other and generate more experiences that you would like to try simply through reading the lists out loud and thinking out loud about more things that would be fun for you.

One person can then volunteer to start this process. I would suggest that the man start this. Pick a time that the 2 of you have some free time. Shiva can pick something from the list and surprise your beloved with it.

The idea here is not to make the most ideal experience happen, but to get into the habit of surprising your beloved with the gift of your attention and your interest in spending time to create and participate in a sexual adventure. Be light hearted about this and have fun. Stay open and flexible to trying something new. Tell each other what you liked about the experience after you've shared this. Also, talk about what you learned about yourself and each other from this experience and what you might want to change for next time.

The other partner can plan the next experience. Continue this process on a weekly basis. Have fun and enjoy the ride!

Exercise 7: Kissing Exercise

Each person take turns and show the other one just how you like to be kissed by kissing the other one in just the way that turns you on the most. Do not tell your partner what you don't like about how they kiss you, but show them in a very detailed way exactly what you like most and teach them to kiss you in that way by showing them. Then ask them to do this and direct them as to how to do this in the way that feels best to you.

When you give your partner direction, tell them first what you like about what they are doing, and then ask them to change if there is something that they could be doing differently. Guide them with your hands or with your mouth or tongue. Give them lots of encouragement about how they are pleasing you and how much pleasure you are receiving through their kisses. Be light-hearted and exaggerate your pleasure as a way of really encouraging your partner to go for pleasing you in a big way.

Reverse roles and do the same thing again. After you are done, talk about what you learned and thank your partner for their participation in this. Talk about what you would like to integrate into your regular lovemaking.

Exercise 8: Playing King & Queen for a Day

This is a fun experience in giving and receiving. Set aside an hour or 2 for each of you. Have one person be the King or Queen. The other person is to meet their every request with love, respect, and acceptance. The idea is to treat your beloved as your king or queen and give them loving and devoted attention. Do what you can to meet their every wish.

Creative Play Exercises

The partner who is the king or queen can ask for whatever they want within reason. Examples would be a massage, a dance that your partner does for you, a hike, taking you out to dinner or fixing a sensuous dinner at home, dressing up in special sexy clothes. Use your creative imagination to cook up the most pleasurable experiences possible to request. The partner who is giving has a right to say no to anything that does not fit or does not feel right or within their boundaries. If you say no, be willing to give an alternative of something you think would work for you that might be just as fun. Discuss this until you can come up with something that is pleasing to the designated king or queen.

When the person has their turn at being king or queen, set the stage by showering, dressing up to look your best, and then bowing to your partner, saying namaste, and showering her or him with your attention and love. Treat him or her as if they are a true king or queen deserving of your deep love and attention and devotion. Be light hearted about this, but also very sensitive to your partner's needs and their feelings. This can be a very delicate experience if you or your partner is not used to giving or being given to in this way.

Once you have shared this, process how it felt to each of you and what you learned about yourself and each other. You can reverse roles and do the same thing again or you can save the giving to the other partner for another time. Be sure to allow at least an hour for this and more if you can create the time.

Exercise 9: Sharing Your Joys & Sorrows

This communication exercise can be done at dinner or during any free time when you want to communicate in a deep way. Decide who will be the giver of information and who will be the receiver. The giver starts with something that has been joyful or happy for them. They can spend as much time as they want telling you about it. You can ask questions to draw them out or get more information. The receiver of information can be as complementary as possible and as upbeat as possible to celebrate the success that the giver of information has had.

Once they are done, you can ask them for a sorrow or a problem or a complaint that they have. If they have a complaint, it's important that they bring a suggested solution to solve the problem or the complaint that they have. This helps the conversation to not stay negative, but to end with something that can be done about the complaint.

Once the giver is done, reverse roles. When both of you have completed sharing, talk about how you felt about this exercise and what you learned about yourself and each other.

Exercise 10: Creating a Win-Win Solution

This skill is helpful to create compromises when there are differences of opinion or when there is a conflict. Instead of using the old model of having to get your way and exclude the other one from getting their way, think of a way that you both can win in the situation. This means that you keep in mind that both of you count and both of you deserve to get your needs met in this situation.

Creative Play Exercises

Keep in mind that your partner loves you as much as himself or herself and wants the best for you just like you want the best for her or him. With this in mind, hold out for a solution that works for the both of you. This may not mean that the solution is the one that you would necessarily choose if your were doing this by yourself. However, the solution needs to be one that you can both live with and feel comfortable with.

Please understand that this process may seem cumbersome at first since you may not be familiar with this. People may not see a solution that meets both people's needs. However, stay with this. Look at the underlying needs below what the apparent solutions are. Stick with this until a solution becomes apparent that works for both of you.

Exercise 11: Tell Me Who You Are

This is a great exercise to do daily that can help people communicate in an intimate and open and loving way even if they don't have a lot of time.

Decide who will be the talker and who will be the listener. The listener's role is to listen with an open heart and pay close attention to what the talker is saying. Also notice what you are thinking and feeling as the talker shares their experience. The listener is not to say anything, but to maintain eye contact and be attentive.

The talker can talk about their feelings, desires, physical sensations and behaviors. AS the talker, try to stay away from thoughts about something else or someone else. Talk about yourself and your own personal experience. Using I messages will help with this.

Once the talker is finished, the listener says thank you and you can then reverse roles.

Once you have both completed this exercise, talk about how you felt about the exercise and what you learned. This exercise is a unique and different form of communication because there is not the back and forth cross talk. This communication style focuses on one person at a time. It is a good style to use during conflicts. When you are using it to resolve conflict, decide which person is most upset or feeling the strongest about the situation. They become the talker and share their experience until they feel complete. Then you can reverse roles.

Creative Play Exercises

Expressing Anger Constructively

The following is an excellent model of expressing anger constructively. It is based on the 3 stages of anger. The 1st stage is the fiery stage of anger where our energy for fighting and striking out at the other is very strong. Many times, this is when we say and do things we regret later. This is a good time to take a time out, be alone and center ourselves. During this time, we can express our energy physically through screaming, crying, pounding on a pillow, hitting a punching bag or getting physical exercise. The focus here is getting the energy out and understanding what our deep feelings and needs are. Writing a letter not to be sent to the person we are angry at, but using it to express our feelings and understand our needs and learn how to take responsibility to get our needs met is the point of this letter. The following is a format for the letter:

Dear_____,

I'm angry about
I'm sad/ hurt about
I'm afraid of
What I regret is
What I deserved then and now is
What I appreciate about me, about you is
What I want now is
What I'm willing to do to get what I want is...
What I'm learning about myself from this situation is

Love,

Me

Write an ideal response letter from the person you are upset with. Two things happen when you do this. You nurture yourself with hearing what you want to hear from the other person (the right brain where emotional healing happens doesn't know the difference between imagination and reality). Also, you get clear about what you really want from the other person. You can then communicate much more clearly to the other person what it is you want.

The 2nd stage of constructive anger management is to communicate what you are feeling and what you need. The way to do this is to take the letter that you wrote and re-write it in a caring way so that you can share your feelings with your partner in a way they can hear and receive. This is also an important time to plan how this will not happen again and to agree on changes each of you will make for prevention. Once each person acknowledges how they will act to prevent this happening in the future, the way is paved for an apology, forgiveness and gratitude.

The 3rd stage is making up. This is a time for cuddling, holding each other, re-establishing the closeness that was lost. It also can be an important time to share gratitude for having gotten through a rough time and gratitude for your beloved partner.

This is the end of these exercises. The goodbye I would like to offer you is one I have used in spiritual groups for many years.

> "May the Circle be open, but unbroken. May the love of each other be always in our hearts. Merry meet, and merry part, and merry meet again."

I would love your feedback as to how the exercises helped you or what more you would like to integrate sex, love and spirit into your every day life. Feel free to write me at lovingwaydiana@gmail.com to tell me your responses to my book.

Blessings on your path.

Namaste,

Diana

Bibliography

A.H. Almaas. Various works. www.ridhwan.org.

Anand, Margot. *The Art of Everyday Ecstasy*, Broadway Books, New York, NY, 1998.

Anand, Margot. *The Art of Sexual Ecstasy*, Jeremy P. Tarcher, Los Angeles, CA, 1989.

Anand, Margot. *Sexual Ecstasy, The Art of Orgasm, Exercises from the Art of Sexual Magic*, Jeremy P. Tarcher/Putnam, New York, NY, 2000.

Anand, Margot. *The Sexual Ecstasy Workbook, The Path of Sky Dancing Tantra*, Jeremy P. Tarcher/Putnam, 2005.

Foley, Sallie; Kope, Sally A; Sugrue, Dennis P. *Sex Matters For Women*, The Guilford Press, New York, NY, 2002.

Heumann, Suzie and Campbell, Susan. *The Everything Great Sex Book*, Adams Media, Avon, Massachusetts, 2004.

Judith, Anodea and Vega, Selene. *The Sevenfold Journey, Reclaiming Mind, Body & Spirit Through the Chakras*, The Crossing Press, Freedom, CA, 1993.

Kuriansky, Dr. Judy. *The Complete Idiot's Guide to Tantric Sex*, Alpha Books, Indianapolis, IN, 2002.

Bibliography

Richardson, Diana. *Tantric Orgasm for Women*, Destiny Books, Rochester, VT, 2004.

Williamson, Marianne. *Illuminated Prayers*, Simon & Schuster, New York, NY, 1997.

Yarian, David. Various works. www.DavidYarian.com

Zilbergeld, Bernie. *Male Sexuality*, Bantam Books, New York, NY, 1981.

Zilbergeld, Bernie. *The New Male Sexuality*, Bantam Books, New York, NY, 1993.

VIDEOS

Margot Anand's *Secret Keys to the Ultimate Love Life* (DVD Trilogy)

Margot Anand's *The Art of Orgasm For Men & Women* (2-DVD Set)

Tantric Yoga for Lovers by Steve and Lokita Carter

The Breath of Tantric Love with Steve and Lokita Carter

Tantric Massage for Lovers with Steve and Lokita Carter

To purchase any of these videos, visit www.tantra.com.

www.ingramcontent.com/pod-product-compliance
Lightning Source LLC
LaVergne TN
LVHW081317060426
835509LV00015B/1563